AROUND BRITAIN
BY CANAL

AROUND BRITAIN BY CANAL

1,000 Miles of Waterways

Anthony Burton

PEN & SWORD
TRANSPORT

AN IMPRINT OF PEN & SWORD BOOKS LTD.
YORKSHIRE – PHILADELPHIA

For Pip, Jenny and Nicholas,
who were left behind

First published in Great Britain in 2018 by
PEN & SWORD TRANSPORT
An imprint of
Pen & Sword Books Ltd
Yorkshire - Philadelphia

Copyright@ Anthony Burton, 2018

ISBN 978 1 47389 323 8

Typeset in 10/13.5 Palatino
Typeset by Aura Technology and Software Services, India
Printed and bound in India by Replika Press Pvt. Ltd.

Pen & Sword Books Ltd incorporates the Imprints of Pen & Sword Books Archaeology,
Atlas, Aviation, Battleground, Discovery, Family History, History, Maritime, Military,
Naval, Politics, Railways, Select, Transport, True Crime, Fiction, Frontline Books, Leo
Cooper, Praetorian Press, Seaforth Publishing, Wharncliffe and White Owl.

For a complete list of Pen & Sword titles please contact

PEN & SWORD BOOKS LTD
47 Church Street, Barnsley, South Yorkshire, S70 2AS, England
E-mail: enquiries@pen-and-sword.co.uk
Website: www.pen-and-sword.co.uk

Or
PEN AND SWORD BOOKS
1950 Lawrence Rd, Havertown, PA 19083, USA
E-mail: Uspen-and-sword@casematepublishers.com
Website: www.penandswordbooks.com

Contents

Preface

This journey took place at a time when the large-scale restoration of the canal system had only achieved a fraction of what was to be accomplished in later years. Had I been making the trip today, I could have chosen two alternative routes across the Pennines, on either the Rochdale or Huddersfield Canals, but would I think still prefer the Leeds & Liverpool. The southern route could have been extended, were I brave enough to take a narrow boat along the tidal Severn and the Avon, by using the beautiful Kennet & Avon. But on the whole, I think I would be happy with the chosen route. Perhaps the most startling difference between then and now is how attitudes have changed towards canals in cities. The Birmingham canals, once generally thought of in terms of dead dogs and supermarket trolleys, are now lined with fashionable restaurants and bars and who could have imagined that the Rochdale Canal in Manchester would now be associated with a thriving gay scene? The other notable change has been the decline of canalside industry and the end of such distinctive features as the still busily working Tom Puddings of the north. So, in many ways, this has become a historical document, rather than an account of everything that might be seen on a similar trip today. One thing, however, remains unchanged: the constant fascination of a journey by canal, which is what the book was always meant to attempt to capture.

New technology has had one beneficial effect on publishing: it has now become much more economical to produce books with colour illustrations. Fortunately, Phillip Lloyd who was with me for the whole journey was an enthusiastic and gifted photographer. As a result, instead of being illustrated by a few black and white photos, the book has now blossomed in full colour. I am most grateful to Phillip for allowing me to use his photos. Advances in technology have not all been good news. Because so many books are now ordered online, it has become necessary to include key words in the title that will show up on search engines. The book was originally called "Back Door Britain", a title that is explained in the first chapter – it has been changed to meet the new requirements, but the ethos remains the same. The canal system still offers a view of the country that you will never get by any other means of transport.

Anthony Burton
Stroud, 2018

CHAPTER 1

On Back Doors

When I was young, one of the great treats was to be taken to stay with my grandmother in Stockton-on-Tees. Like most such recollections my own are made up of a mixture of very sharp images, where every detail comes out precise and highly coloured, and the vaguer pictures, that become little more than a blurred alternation of days when the sun shone with a brilliance we have never seen since, or the rain fell in sheets. In childhood memories there is no place for the merely dull. Clearest of all the memories comes the kitchen at the back of the house: the feel of it, the warmth from the big fire at the kitchen range, where the kettle hissed permanently on the hob; the smell of bread cooking; and the sight of it, a comforting warmth of colours, battered brown leather chairs, lino cloth on the table, brown velvet curtains worn to a threadbare golden old age. It was all as snug and cosy as a well-lined nest. Life in that house revolved around the kitchen. Here I played in muzzy comfort on the dark, wet days, and they are the days I remember best. The kitchen world was cut off from the rest of the house by the heavy, draught-defying curtain which came in so useful for amateur theatricals, when I mounted supremely egotistic one-boy shows for long-suffering relations.

There was another door out of the kitchen – the back door that led to the outside world. There was no curtain hanging there, for it was in constant use. In memory, neighbours are for ever poking their heads round that door, looking round the busy kitchen scene before asking the ritual question: 'Anyone at home?' Beyond the back door was the other part of that childhood back-of-the-house memory, the yard; a cobbled area surrounded by a high wall, ideal for ball games. The smell of the yard that comes back is of mint and washing – in equal parts. There was so little soil in the yard, there was room for nothing to grow apart from the wiry mint plants; the wash-house was out in the yard, steam-filled each Monday when clothes were pounded in a great galvanized tub. And beyond the yard wall was the back alley and the corner shop. It was by that alley wall that I first began to find pleasure in seeing how ingenious men could be, for it contained a device which, even as a child, impressed me by its magnificently effective simplicity. This was a hinged trapdoor let into the wall, through which you could dump all the household rubbish. A second trap, set lower down, allowed the dustman to empty it straight out the other side. I can still recall with pleasure the sight of the alley walls of Stockton disgorging themselves into the Corporation cart.

The house had a front door and stood facing other houses across the street; but that was the dull, formal part of the world. The front door was for Ministers of Religion and the Man from the Pru, who knocked and waited to be allowed in. And the front room was for tea from the best china and polite conversation and chintz on the chairs. It was always Sunday in the front room. The family that sat around in the front room did not seem to be quite the same family that worked in the back. As a child, I preferred the world at the back of the house. On more mature reflection I still do.

The main street of Stockton is wide enough to take the Town Hall and a market in the centre, with ample room for traffic on either side. Market days bring bright, bustling memories, but otherwise it seems, to my mind's eye, less colourful, with the glorious exception of the department store at the end of the street, where change whistled all round the shop in shining metal cylinders. I was, I suppose, adolescent before I discovered that the town also had a back door world, the world of the river, which in those days still had its shipyards and boats. It had a very different air about it. It was all rather shabbier, dirtier, but yet had a unique atmosphere made by the tall warehouses ranged along narrow streets that suddenly opened up to the wide river scene. As a child I responded instinctively to these atmospheres. I don't believe I ever stopped to think out how the town had grown up around its importance as an inland port, but I was conscious of the difference, aware that a town could have two quite distinct personalities. The town was not so very different from the house in Richmond Road.

Today I travel the country a good deal, usually by car. I seem to reach more places but see less, and what I do see from the main road is the front door world. This book is about a journey I made to find the other side of village, town and city. Such a journey had to meet a number of requirements. First, I had to travel to the right sorts of areas. That was essential. Then I had to have a form of transport that would give me time to see the world around me and it had to be a form of travel that I would actually enjoy. There was only one that matched my needs. There are any number of ways of moving around the country that give you time. You can ride a horse, but you can hardly ride your nag through the middle of Birmingham. Or you can go by bicycle, but that fell foul of the other criterion, that I should enjoy it. Or you can walk.

Alas, I am too lazy. For me the choice was simple. I would travel the country by canal.

The canals are one of the great loves of my life, and no route could be more aptly described as back door than a canal route. You scarcely see anything else. Built to serve industry, canals tend to sidle up on towns, creeping in among the mills and factories, emerging only briefly to peer at the more fashionable areas before scurrying off again. Speed is absolutely perfect: you are not even allowed to go faster than four miles an hour. Nothing could be better, nothing more appropriate and certainly nothing more enjoyable. And the route was quite easily fixed. I wanted to do a continuous tour with as little doubling-up as possible, and to cover as wide an area as I could. It was simple enough, but I spent what seemed like months going over and over the details and schedules. At last, with a sublime disregard for superstition, I set off on 13 March 1975- to collect the 45'-foot narrow boat *Water Columbine*. My back door journey had begun.

CHAPTER 2

The Heart of England

The journey began at Hillmorton, on the outskirts of Rugby. Arriving by car, you drive through the suburban streets until you reach one, much the same as all the others, called Brindley Road in deference to the great canal engineer. That's enough to tell you that you are nearly there. Down the road, through the narrow tunnel that pierces the railway embankment and out the other side to the canal, a visual change as startling as the move from the dark into the light. From suburbia you've reached the countryside; from the modern housing estate you have turned back two hundred years to the old Oxford Canal and the Canal Company buildings. Here, right at the start, are many of the special qualities that draw me back to the canal time and time again. Here is a group of buildings that belong completely to one moment in time and, just as importantly, to one region. Hillmorton Yard is a good place to set up a few standards.

Hillmorton is close to the very centre of England, and the buildings are as essentially English as any you could find. Here in Warwickshire you are in brick country. Coming as I do from the North of England, I am always inclined to look down on brick as a second-class building material. Stone is the thing. Brick buildings, like thirties semis elbowing their way in between the old, dark houses of local gritstone, are intrusions. But what I saw then was the stock brick, as different from these local bricks as concrete is from stone. Here the bricks were fired locally, formed from the red clay. And they have a richness of colour and texture that is hard to match today. In the days when these bricks were made, kiln temperatures tended to be a bit hit and miss, so you get a whole variety of colours from the deepest red to a lightish brown. And they have one great virtue: they improve with age, seeming to retreat back to fit in with the natural colours of the countryside from which they came.

The buildings themselves are plain enough, built to serve a purpose, quiet and functional. It is a simple grouping: the office, looking like a respectable, middle-class house, stands next to the lock, while the maintenance buildings are tucked away on a side arm, behind the high, rounded arch of the old bridge. There is nothing elaborate, no decoration. So why is it so satisfying to look at? Partly, it is just the presence of the water. Any building set down by water gains something in interest from the shifting reflections and the play of light. Partly, too, the answer lies with a feeling of right proportions, that unmistakable hallmark of Georgian building. But for me, the main joy lies in this feeling that the buildings belong in their surroundings, belong to this one particular place. It is a quality to which, I believe, most people respond, even if it is only subconsciously. Here are buildings that sit squarely and most comfortably in an old tradition of British architecture.

Nowadays, Hillmorton is the base for part of the British Waterways Board (B.W.B.) fleet of hire boats, and it was here, after leaving the car with no regrets whatsoever, that I collected the boat that was to be home for the next six weeks. The old working boatman would have recognized the 45"-foot steel hull as having a strong family resemblance to the traditional narrow boat, but inside in the cabin, it would have seemed a dream of almost unimaginable luxury. Hire boats such as this, built at Market Harborough, are specially designed for the holiday trade, and very well designed at that. They come complete with central heating, hot and cold running water, shower, cooker, fridge and a device known as a pump-out toilet, which was to prove something less than an unmixed blessing. Starting at the front, there is the water tank in the bows, and the first cabin, which the nautically inclined call the saloon, though it has always seemed to me a bit pompous to use language more appropriate to an ocean-going yacht. It's the place where you can sit down or have a meal, and it comes complete with a seat that makes into a double bed for the night. Beyond that is the kitchen. Then there are two more cabins, each with two bunks and wash basins. The stern is the business end of the boat, where there is an open deck over the diesel engine, and the tiller and controls. People new to the canals are often nervous of this type of boat. They tend to look instead to the fibre-glass cruiser with wheel steering, something that seems more like the friendly family car. It is a mistake. The steel-hulled narrow boat is, after all, the craft that has grown up with the canals, the end product of two centuries of experience. It won't blow around much in the wind, and the steerer has the whole length of the boat in view. It is so robust, so easy to handle that a child can manage it. In fact my daughter could steer when she was still so small she had to stand on a box to see over the cabin roof. The only thing you have to get used to is remembering which way you have to push the tiller, and learning that the boat pivots around the centre and not around one end.

The former
maintenance yard at Hillmorton, a typical example of attractive yet strictly functional canal architecture.

When everything was stowed away, I was joined by the crew. Crew hardly seems the right word, for it suggests a sort of Captain Bligh hierarchy which, I hope, never materialized. Anyway, whatever you want to call them, they came: Phil and Bill. It sounds like a music-hall act and, as far as appearance is concerned, they would have made a good pair: Phil, tall, blond and thin; Bill, short, dark and, well, stout. And, just for the day, we were joined by an old friend, Peter White, whose many virtues included an ability to provide an apparently endless supply of food and hot drinks.

I backed the boat down the arm and out into the canal. And, at once, all the familiar pleasures of canal travel were back with me again. The whole pace of your life starts to slow down and take on a new meaning. The day is governed by the light of the sun, not the ticking of a clock on the wall. You could do away with clocks and watches altogether on the canal if it was not for the absurdities of the British licensing laws. You move at a walking pace, and in accepting that pace you seem to be brought closer to the whole natural world: you find yourself becoming more conscious of your surroundings, aware of quite small changes in the land about you, in the weather, in the movements of animals and birds. You have a sense that man is just another animal with his own place in the order of things. But you are also conscious of the great changes that man has made, of how he has set his mark on even the most natural-seeming landscapes.

The day was grey, with a chill, clinging dampness that lingered on through the morning. We seemed to move through an oddly monochrome land, as if we were being pictured in a faded sepia print. The water was ochre-ish, bounded by grey straggles of trees and brambles, still leafless and coloured only with the dull green of moss. The fields beyond were, at first, only snatched glimpses of a brighter green. Even the bird life seemed to fit into this mood. The heron stands like a grey, cast-iron ornament, waiting until the very last minute, when the bows of the boat are almost level with him, before taking off with a lazy beat of wide wings, his long neck tucked into his shoulders. He is like a flying wedge. The heron is a bird that takes a dim view of the passing boats. He flies up, moves on ahead and resumes his game of statues. But the wretched boat keeps coming on, disturbing him again, and he keeps being pushed forward until he tires of the whole business and swings round in a great arc to land back where he started. Sometimes you'll see the heron get a fish: the long neck snakes into the water and the victim is speared and gobbled down in a flash. But mostly, he just stands around, wishing you'd go away.

Other birds seem less concerned by our passing. Coots and moorhen bob in the wake. Pigeons mostly stay out of sight but seldom out of earshot with their hollow, dreary repetition, whoo-hoo-wh, whoo-hoo-wh. In the fields the lapwings scarcely bother to break off from their endless pecking, raising their comma'd heads for a moment, before returning to the feast. Magpies – one for sorrow, two for joy – come out in ones to remind us the date is the thirteenth. The sun accepts the omen and stays behind the clouds.

Travelling down this part of the Oxford Canal, you may not notice man's intrusion, but it's there all right. It is there in the canal itself. The centuries have worked at smoothing out what was once a raw scar on the countryside, but they cannot disguise the fact that the canal wrought a major change, marked the beginning of a new age. This part of the country probably offers more extensive evidence of the old, medieval pattern of farming than any other. Not that it was the canal that brought a change to farming methods. That came long before, with the Black Death, when the population drastically declined. There just weren't enough people around to work the land and much of the old arable went over to pasture for sheep. But the old patterns still stayed on the ground. The medieval peasant had farmed his strip, ploughing up and down the full length of it with a plough that dug deep furrows and threw up high ridges, and each strip was marked from its neighbour with a double furrow. That old field system meant nothing to the canal engineer, cutting through the land, looking for a level not a medieval boundary. So the canal today slices straight through ridge and furrow, giving the traveller a cross-section view, an instant lesson in agricultural history.

Canal travel is punctuated with pleasant regularity by bridges. They act as identification marks and distance posts: a bridge number and a map are all you need to keep a check on progress. The old bridges are built of the mellow brick found at Hillmorton, yet it was along the same canal that the materials of the new age were brought. Builders were no longer limited by what they could find at their own doorsteps. Some materials were introduced because they were better, most because they were cheaper. And, once begun, the pace of change accelerated and you can measure that change from the bridges you meet along the way. Where the railway crosses the canal, you find a structure very different from the little humpbacked bridge that is no more than a ripple on the horizon. The railway comes up on a high bank and crosses on a massive bridge. Though it is still made of brick, it is quite alien. This is the blue engineering brick, which became as typical of the modern industrial regions of the Midlands as the red brick was typical of the old rural areas.

The material may have changed, but the railway bridge was still just a canal bridge writ large, based on the powerful but visually satisfying contrast between straight parapet and curved arch. The twentieth century has changed all that. Brick has given way to concrete; the arch has been replaced by the slab. Most people, if asked, will say they prefer the old bridges, and I would suggest they are reacting against two new factors: the modern bridge is all straight lines, which are at odds with the curve of the land, and the material it is built from has no relation to the natural materials of the country. The old brick goes back closer to its origins; the concrete gets grubbier. Yet, there is a consolation, for even the motorway bridge now plays a part in the life of the countryside. The wire fence that runs as a boundary under the bridge makes an ideal backscratcher for sheep sheltering from the rain. I dare say you could pick enough wool to knit a sweater if you had a mind to it.

Look at a map, and the half dozen or so miles from Hillmorton to Braunston look singularly dull, and so they are if you are looking for some overwhelming excitement. There are no great monuments, no marvellous engineering features, not even any towns, but once you have got the habit of looking it is anything but dull. For me the pleasure was the keener simply because it was my first day back on the canal after nearly a year away. Certainly there is an egotistical pleasure in sliding the boat accurately, without a single bump, into that first lock. You take it much more seriously the first time; the bumps will come later. Then you have the opportunity to look around, note details. Pen goes to notebook with astonishing regularity. A plain, square, red-brick Georgian house becomes special precisely because you are looking; it is this act of looking that makes the building into something special, that makes you aware of the details. Passing just such a house I noticed the changing style of the brick work. There is often a sort of checkered effect on the houses. This is produced by the use of Flemish bond, where stretchers (bricks laid with their side to the wall face) and headers (bricks laid so that the ends are seen) alternate. Use different coloured bricks for headers and stretchers and you have diaper work of a chequerboard pattern. No need to know the technical names, but it is worthwhile seeing what a wealth of variety you can find in the simplest buildings.

The Oxford Canal joins the Grand Union at Braunston, a village that climbs the hill to the church at the summit. It is a very grand looking church for such a small place, topped by a tall spire and a myriad of pinnacles, that suggest either early English Gothic or Victorian: in this case both, as it was restored to what it never was by Butterfield in the 1870s. The canal at the bottom of the hill takes no notice of such extravagance but makes its own small world. The actual junction arrives with a pair of cast-iron bridges which with their low graceful arches stand as irrefutable evidence that materials such as iron and techniques of mass production need not result in ugliness. The simple beauty has nothing whatsoever to do with decoration and embellishment, and everything to do with form. These are practical solutions to practical problems, and just the thing for a busy working area, for Braunston is one of the few places where the traditional narrow boats of the canal carry on with their trade. You can see them in these winter months, loaded with the cargo that was the mainstay of the whole canal system for two hundred years – coal. Not so long ago, a working narrow boat was about as romantic as a coal lorry. Now that their working days have come to an end, we stop and admire, click away with our cameras and sigh for the good old days. A floating coal merchant is only a floating coal merchant, but I wallow in nostalgia with the rest.

The near empty landscape changed little as we veered away south-west towards Napton Hill, crowned by its sail-less windmill like some phallic offering to a pagan god. This is the first major turning point.

The simple brick bridge that joins the basin at Hillmorton yard to the Oxford Canal.

The old Oxford Canal swings sharply off to the south, while we followed the Grand Union to begin our trek up north. It was here that we had our first glimpse of a problem that was to plague us for much of the trip – the water shortage. The reservoirs were ominously low after a dry winter. People often look at the still waters of a canal and imagine that all you have to do is fill it with water and leave it, just topping up occasionally to take care of leaks. Would it were that simple. Every time you go through a lock on the Grand Union, you are shifting over 5-0,000 gallons of water. Moving downhill you push that 50,000 gallons in front of you all the time, until at last you shove it right out of the canal. There lies the problem, which is why, in times of water shortage, the authorities are happy to see you cruise all day up and down the pounds – the stretches of water between locks – but impose restrictions on the use of the locks themselves.

For the time being, the locks were open, and we had a mildly energetic afternoon with a dozen locks to work, three at Calcutt and another nine at Stockton. I like locks. I enjoy the physical effort and I especially enjoy working a flight efficiently and well. In part, I suppose, it is a reaction against a sedentary life which offers little more energetic than pushing a pen over a page. But there is also the romance of it all: in his heart of hearts, every canal enthusiast sees himself as a working boatman, in spirit if not in fact. We tell ourselves that we are working the locks as well as any working boatman – which we seldom are – and invest our boating with a kind of mystique. We worry about ludicrous matters like getting the names of boats right. The boats in these parts are narrow boats – barges are quite different, they are wide boats. Oh, we are all so quick to correct the ignorant who call our narrow boats barges. I once asked an old boatman what he called his boat. He replied – and I give a bowdlerized version – 'my bloody boat'. But we retain our fantasies and they harm no one.

Stockton locks mark a change in the canal scene: a temporary halt to the open rural landscape, and the first appearance of industry. Even if you failed to recognize the cement works as such, you could still make a fair guess at what goes on in this part of the world by looking at a few local names. Canal bridge 20 is called Gibraltar Bridge – Gibraltar, rock. The pub is the Blue Lias, and blue lias is a type of stone. No great deductive logic needed to work out that this area is quarried for blue lias.

The end of the locks also marked the end of work for the day, and we moored outside the Two Boats Inn and finished the day inside it. Canal travel is not only punctuated by bridges and locks, it is also, praise be, punctuated by pubs. The pub plays an important part in canal travel. When you moor for the night near a small village or out in the country, the pub is the one social centre you can rely on, the one escape from the slightly cramped conditions of the boat, not to mention the faces you have been staring at all day. But even without such special circumstances, I do like good pubs and good beer, and I did like the Two Boats. It is plain and homely, not gaudy and impersonal. A log fire roared in the elaborately carved fireplace, and the landlord talked to his customers: the local pub is one of the last bastions to be held for the art of conversation, a place where the supposedly reserved English do actually talk to complete strangers. The pub is due for modernization, which means that the log fire will be no more, and one can only hope that it will not mean the loss of the genuine local atmosphere. It is a sad commentary on our times that the very word modernization now seems darkly ominous. But that did not affect us that evening. And so, worn out by fresh air and exercise, and comforted with flagons, to bed.

The next day was as grey as the last. The air leaked a rain too fine to see, a dampness that oozed from the clouds. It was as bleak as November, a salutary warning that winter was officially still with us. No one, however, had warned the lambs. Tottering and vulnerable, bleating for their mas, they must have wondered why they ever left the warm and cosy safety of the womb.

Even the dankest of cold, dank Sundays does nothing to deter the anglers who line the bank, staring with impassive faces at the motionless, muddy water. Anglers are far and away the largest group of canal users. There are thousands upon thousands of them. Yet in all the years I have travelled the canals, I have never once seen an angler catch anything at all. I imagine they must, but I have never seen them, and I often wonder if they even care, or whether they merely take delight in their solitary broodings. I do not know, for angling is a closed book to me, an impenetrable mystery. So we passed them by with a noiseless nod of acknowledgement, leaving each other to our own pleasures, our own thoughts.

Travelling these country routes, one quickly develops a strong sense of the past, for the routes and their surroundings seem to have changed so little with time. One point which is very apparent is the importance of the parish church, if only because it is such a prominent landmark, a physical focus round which the village grouped. The tower or spire must once have been welcome signposts to the older canal traveller, dominating the skyline. At Radford Semele, the church pokes up above a hillside of rich, arable land, lording it over the whole village and even over the Jacobean manor house. The church may have lost its place as the centre of community life, but it still remains a uniquely imposing structure in the rural landscape. If one day we decide to try and make a new focus I only hope we can produce something half as attractive as the plainest of parish churches.

Once past Radford Semele, you start sneaking up on Leamington Spa, past a new housing estate. It is really quite a good estate, with variety and a sense of style – good enough, in fact, to make you wish it was that much better. The main building material is a liverish yellow brick, rather ugly and quite at odds with the traditional material of the area. Seeing an estate such as this from our rather specialized viewpoint, one question inevitably comes up: why not acknowledge that the canal is there. Some of the houses do face out towards the water, although others skulk behind high brick walls, but all are shut away behind spiky iron railings. A small girl was feeding the swans as best she could between the spikes. Those railings will never stop her reaching the water, but they will most effectively stop any adult reaching her should she fall in. So here is the canal with passing boats, swans, ducks, shifting reflections, and still they turn houses to face each other so that the occupant of one house has a superb view of the identical house opposite. Places have their own characteristics, and any good builder will take note of them.

Moored next to the bank, the boat that was to take us on our thousand mile trip round the canals.

After the estate, there's a brief glimpse of an older country building, with farmhouse and duckpond. That sounds good and romantic, but if you want to see a thorough mess made of a group of buildings look at your average farmyard – odd bits of corrugated iron cobbled together, asbestos sheets banged up into a shed. Any old junk that comes to hand will serve. The countryman has little enough cause to feel smug at the expense of his urban neighbours.

So to Leamington. Royal Leamington. Well, there's not much royal about it seen from this end. The canal comes in past terraces of small houses, many of which are derelict and bricked up. The people who live here have made an effort to brighten up the general air of pervading gloom – brickwork has been prinked out with colour wash, woodwork is bright with fresh paint. It reminded me of the marvellous technicolour rows that straddle across the valleys of South Wales. And in among the regimented rows, one can find the quirky bits: the local school, replete with decorative tiles, odd pinnacles and towers. It all looks rather fun, though it is probably rather less fun for those who have to try and teach there. It does, though, have the virtue that it looks as if it has something to do with people and has not been built for the manufacture of transistorized yo-yos. Then we met a real, one-hundred-per-cent oddity. At the end of one of those little Victorian terraces, a house has been Done Up. The courtyard by the canal has been whitewashed and decked out with statuary like a Chelsea mews cottage, and moored alongside is a gondola, not full size perhaps, but a Venetian gondola none the less. It ought all to be absurd, but it is carried off with such panache as to defy criticism.

Going through Leamington by canal, you keep expecting the other more familiar Leamington to put in an appearance. What has happened to the town that has always epitomized gentility and respectability? Where are the tubby villas set smugly in expensive grounds, trying hard to ignore their neighbours? Where is the pump room with its afternoon teas, potted palms and selections from *The Desert Song*? And where, oh where, are all those ladies in flowered hats; where are the haughty accents permanently raised to full volume in training for the next Conservative Party Conference? Wherever they are, they are not down by the canal, which by the time it reaches the middle of the town has nothing more fashionable to offer than its colour, a kind of trendy Habitat khaki, stained by the industry along the banks. Industry? In Leamington? Yes, indeed. There is never any harm in being reminded that all prosperity has to be bought somewhere. But then, hardly has industry appeared before the canal loses it by diving down into a deep cutting, festooned with the inevitable debris and rubbish of urban life. And before you are quite aware that it has happened, Leamington has come and gone and Warwick has gone with it. Lovely place, Warwick, with its fine old castle, the river, the grand entrance gates, but there was no time to stop. Those time restrictions were creeping up on us and we had to leave the city without even a glimpse of its splendours. We were about to begin the climb up to Birmingham.

CHAPTER 3

Brummagem

One thing you can say about canal travel; it is a great teacher of geography. Anyone coming to Birmingham by water soon learns that no matter which way you come, it is all up hill, up hill, up hill. To reach the Birmingham plateau you have to work.

The immediate objective was to get through Hatton locks before they closed down for the night. As the official closing hour was four p.m., I thought we should have no difficulty whatsoever in making it in time. I had not, though, reckoned on the officials working to a rule that said a boat must be out of the flight – the whole series of locks – by four. They closed the locks about an hour and a half before, so that when we arrived at three, the padlocks were in place-deep gloom all round. However, the appearance of the lock keeper brought a touch of hope, and with much persuasive chat and waving of official papers, we were allowed to go on our way up Hatton. There is, I discovered, a great potency in the name 'Melbury House', the headquarters of B.W.B. We seemed to be endlessly repeating it like some magic incantation. 'Melbury House, Melbury House' – it opens all doors, unfastens all locks.

I promised the lock keeper that we should do our best to be up the flight by four. Those who know Hatton will appreciate what a daunting task that is, but for others perhaps a short explanation will make it plain. This is what happens at a lock. We were travelling up hill. If the lock is empty, you can just push the gate open and take the boat straight in. Invariably, due to the operation of Mr Sod's well-known law, the lock will turn out to be full, so the first thing to do is empty it. Water is let in and out of the lock through culverts, closed by moveable covers called ground paddles, or through holes in the lock gates, covered by gate paddles. So to empty the lock all you have to do is lift the paddles and let the water out. That's what it says in the book: 'wind up the paddles'. What the book does not indicate is the amount of effort that might be required. With some paddles, you put the windlass to the paddle gear, a flick or two of the wrist, and up it goes; with others you grunt and sweat and strain and heave. In memory, the latter sort seem to predominate. With the lock empty, you can lower the paddles again, put your back to the long balance beam and push the lock gate open. You bring the boat in, close the gates, fill the lock – more winding of gear – then let the boat out and on its way to the next lock, never forgetting to lower all the paddles before you go. That is one lock, but we had a flight to work, all set close together. At Hatton, we had twenty-one broad locks spread out over two miles. You get the best view of Hatton when you travel by train on the London to Birmingham main line, when you can see this monstrous staircase, black and white beam following black and white beam in steady progression up the hillside. Fortunately for us, the route curves, so that at least we did not start with the whole appalling prospect in view.

Three is a good number for working a flight. There's one to steer the boat, leaving the other two to work the paddles. One of the pair looks after the lock the boat is actually in, while the second goes on to set the next lock. It was like a striptease working up Hatton that afternoon. I started off with an anorak and two sweaters, but as the work of running between the locks went on garments were shed, and I reckon a good deal of excess fat was shed as well. And once you're under way and round the first bend, you've got that long procession clearly in sight. It does very little in the way of providing encouragement. I doubt if we'd ever have got up in anything like the hour if we'd not met a couple of Warwick University students, out for a canalside stroll,

Kingswood, where the Grand Union joins the Stratford Canal.

whom we pressed into service. In the end, we finished Hatton in an hour and twenty minutes. I have never worked a flight of locks at that speed before, and I never want to work one at that speed again. Still, when it was all over we had the compensation of a peaceful five miles through wooded cuttings and fields, the little Shrewley tunnel the only interruption to the view. I hope the students, who came along for the ride, found it some sort of consolation for their labours. At least we were through now to Kingswood Junction, the Stratford Canal and the last lap to Birmingham. We had also made it to a well-earned pint and a more than welcome sleep.

The Stratford Canal runs between the Avon at Stratford and the Worcester and Birmingham Canal. We had joined it at the midpoint, which is also a point of some special interest. North of the junction, the canal is simply part of the general canal system, but below that, to the south, it is owned by the National Trust, and thereby hangs a tale which is one of the most important in the recent history of the waterways. For the Stratford Canal had been virtually abandoned, left as just another linear rubbish dump, until volunteers led by the redoubtable David Hutchings set about restoring it for navigation. It was the first scheme of its kind, and its success ensured that other restoration schemes followed. But it is not only for its general importance that the success of the scheme should be celebrated, for the Stratford Canal offers rare delights. As we were forced to wait in the morning for the magic hour of ten when the man with the golden key would come to set us on our way, we had time to take a closer look at some of those delights.

At the junction itself, there is a maintenance yard, offices and a flight of locks stretching away in both directions. Put as baldly as that, there sounds little to enthuse over, beyond a promise of more hard work to come. But the pleasures of such a place are not to be quickly absorbed. First, you must try and envisage the scene as a whole. The yard, with its simple, robust, well-proportioned buildings faces you. To your right, the canal widens to a reedy bay, then pinches in to the tall, strong verticals of the lock gates, with the spiky paddle gear and severe black and white paintwork, all such a contrast to the water and the waving grasses. To your left is another lock, but now a horizontal motif is emphasized as you look down on the length of the chamber with the splayed out beams. Beyond that is the lock cottage, then the canal swings away out of sight. And to complete the whole scene, there is a cluster of narrow boats, homes to a small floating community. It is all very pleasant, but if you have time to look closer, there is still a good deal more to see. Look at the lock cottage for example. Most canal

cottages are simple, no-nonsense buildings in the straightforward vernacular, but on the southern Stratford the cottages are all barrel-vaulted. Various theories have been put forward to explain this design curiosity. The least plausible has it that they were built this way because the job was given to the navvies who only knew how to build tunnels – you can just see the foreman coming up to the diggings, shouting 'Put your shovels down a minute, lads, gaffer wants you to design a house.' More likely, if more prosaic, is the idea that this particular building method cuts down on materials and saves money. Whatever the answer, the cottages are pleasing, and the touch of eccentricity does no harm at all. I think, though, that my real favourites on the Stratford Canal are the little split bridges that span the tails of locks, by the bottom gates. They are really two short bridges cantilevered out from each side, with a slight gap in the middle. Why are they built like that? Well, in the old days, the horse would be pulling the boat along the canal and would plod up to the lock. When it reached the bridge, the tow rope slotted neatly down the middle, saving the boatman the job of unhitching. Today's quaint curiosity turns out to be no more than yesterday's elegant solution to a practical problem.

Musing time ended with the opening of the locks, and work began with a vengeance. This time there were a mere eighteen locks to get up – Birmingham really is an uphill struggle – but we met a new problem: water, or rather the lack of it. We went into the first lock

The split bridge is a feature of the Stratford Canal: it allows the tow rope of a horse drawn boat to pass through the bridge.

cheerfully enough, but came out into a muddy wallow. There is only one thing you can do in such circumstances – let more water down from further up the flight, until you have enough to float you into the lock. It is a long and tedious process, which we had to repeat several times before we got to the top. But we were not the only sufferers. Little fish were left floundering in the mud, and we were politely asked if we would mind taking on hitchhikers – two farm geese had gone down over a weir and could not make the trip back. We were quite happy to share our lock and give them a lift home.

It was a weary plod up that flight and, although time was getting on, I felt that a little refreshment would send us on our way in somewhat better spirits, and the Wharf at Hockley Heath did seem very inviting. It was worth the stopping – a plain pub that offered plain snacks that were just what plain snacks ought to be. I had cheese served up with bread still warm from the local bakery, firm bread, bread with flavour to it. I have never understood why television bread adverts always stress softness and lightness, virtues more appropriate to the cotton wool the wretched products usually taste like. I could not help thinking back to just about the last time I stopped on the Stratford Canal to get something to eat. We were on a family holiday almost exactly a year ago when we reached Lowsonford on what turned out to be half-closing day. We were not too worried, for we thought we would get something to eat at the Fleur de Lys. Well, the Fleur de Lys did have food. It had a choice of sandwiches or pizzas, which sounded fine. The kids were not allowed inside, so we asked for a plateful of sandwiches to take out to the garden. That was when the trouble started: no food could be taken out. We explained the circumstances, but no change. It all became rather like a Victorian melodrama as, with shaking fingers, we pointed to the pinched faces of the children pressed against the window pane. Were they to be sent away hungry? Yes, it appeared they were. Then, a solution was found. The children would of course be allowed into the restaurant if we wanted to eat there. That sounded fine again, so we ordered pizzas all round. Then we met Catch 22. No pizzas in the restaurant, only the special dinner menu – expensive haute cuisine we could not afford, and which the children probably wouldn't have eaten anyway. The evening was saved from total disaster by a group of customers who volunteered to ferry us to another pub where the landlord had not erased the word 'hospitality' from his dictionary. We rounded up the family and went out to a large van, emblazoned with the legend 'Circus'! Our rescuers spent a cheery evening with us, and it all ended with the driver giving a magnificent

At Kings Norton. this unusual guillotine lock marks the end of the Stratford Canal, where it joins the Worcester & Birmingham.

display of fire-eating in the pub car park, to the joy of the children and the alcoholic amazement of another customer who staggered out of the gents in time to see a man blow a ten-foot flame from his mouth and staggered right back in again. So hats off to pubs like the Wharf and bad cess to the Fleur de Lys and all its brethren.

I have always suspected that the English have never completely adapted to an urban life. Given half a chance, they will manufacture their own little bits of countryside, or better still, their own country homes. As you get nearer to Birmingham, odd little chalets appear alongside the canal. Some are very obviously home-made in an astonishing range of materials, from quite respectable planking down to old advertising hoardings banged together in a faded patchwork, full of mysterious, sawn-off slogans. 'Bov is go for y', or 'Thin go bett wit Cok'. Around the ill-kempt buildings are some very well kept gardens, and after all what is a garden but a bit of country carried to town? Perhaps we should preserve more of this country-in-town feeling if we were not quite so anxious to hide our individual patches of greenery away behind hedges and walls.

By the time you reach Yardley Wood, the influence of Birmingham is strong. Along the canal, the red brick gives way before the advance of blue engineering bricks, and the older housing gives way to the worst sort of modern anonymity, housing estates with no local connections – anonymous materials, anonymous styles, laid out on a grid that owes nothing to local geography and everything to the planner's straight edge rule. The canal helped the process to grow. It was along the route we were travelling that Welsh slate first came to replace local tiles, that bricks from the big yards came to replace the locally fired ones. And now we pay the penalty. Plonk people down into this drab nowhereland and you cannot be too surprised if they show little pride in their environment. Along the canal, the trees blossom with a grimy flourish of grey plastic; rubbish collects on the bank before sliding down into the water to wrap itself round the prop. This is the sort of area where you spend an awful lot of time with the weed-hatch up, groping around up to your elbows in dirty, freezing water, trying to untangle the polythene and the wire. We were glad enough to leave it all behind as we passed through Broadwood tunnel, marked at its northern end by a bust of Stratford's favourite son, then up to the junction and the guillotine lock and the canal office that looks like a grand country house. What with the water shortages at Lapworth locks and the plastic bags, the light was already dying as we turned into the Worcester and Birmingham and headed up towards the city centre.

Birmingham is an industrial city, and industry is what you see in the street lights and the strong beam of the boat's headlamp. Factories hiss out steam that collects on the water like mist round Count Dracula's castle – and some of those Gothic Victorian buildings would make good homes for the toothy Transylvanian. Turrets and towers,

Gas Street Basin, Birmingham. When this photo was taken many of the old warehouses had been demolished, but nothing yet put in their place.

some topped by intricate little wrought-iron crowns rise up in dark silhouette against the night sky. Industry has become fantasy. Pipes cross and recross in complex webs, while strange bulbous shapes rise up from them like balloons. Metal works splutter and fume in weird cacophony; sparks jump, hot metal glows rich red through open doors. By day it may all be dull enough and plain enough, but at night it takes on a splendour of its own.

The industrial scene is not all fantastic. Even seen from the outside, the Bournville works can be recognized as a model of good order and an almost puritanical cleanliness. In the well lit rooms white-coated, white-hatted men are to be seen, looking for all the world as if they are just off to the next appendicectomy. But chocolate is what it is all about, as the sickly smell that wafts over the water soon reminds you. Opposite the factory are the wharves that were once busy with boats, a reminder of just how much of Birmingham's prosperity was built on the canal system. For Birmingham was its hub, and those with a taste for useless statistics might like to contemplate the fact that Birmingham has more miles of canal than Venice.

As industry is left behind Birmingham University appears, at night as strange and intriguing as the hissing factories. The skyline is dominated by the minaret-like clock tower, and by the vast greenhouses, like well lit pleasure domes, that glow in the dark. Under the arc lamps, the plants are developing, just as though they, too, must be forced to assume the nature of artefacts, before they can be allowed to take their place in such an aggressively urban environment. Beyond is one of the few high-rise developments in Birmingham that has real quality, that relates to and makes use of the landscape. Here the buildings are grouped around one of the old fish ponds. What a difference water makes, taking the harsh outline of a tall building, and repeating it as a gently wavering curve. The lights along the driveway stagger in multiple reflection like the decorative lights of a fair ground, and even as the trees cut off the view, the water is still visible as odd glimpses of lamp glow or an oily, shifting blackness.

We slipped into Edgbaston tunnel, gliding on water so still that it provided a complete, unbroken reflection and we seemed to be floating into the centre of a cylinder. Once out on the other side we were in the heart of the city, passing under Broad Street with its familiar stumpy spire of the Unitarian Church and round to Farmer's Bridge to moor for the night outside the Long Boat. Brummagem at last.

The Long Boat is part of a development that has tried to make use of the canal, keeping the essentially robust character of the area, but

making it accessible to a lot more people, not just those in boats. In many ways it has been successful, and the pub is certainly part of the success. The builders have not attempted a slavish copying of a traditional canal pub, but have gone back to first principles. What makes a good pub? The obvious answer is good beer, but that's something the builders can't control, so we'll look at some of the other factors. The first thing a pub needs to be is robust. I know pubs where they've put in delicate chairs, hung flowered wallpaper and set frilly curtains up at the windows. They're places where you feel you have to talk in a whisper and to ask for anything as common as a pint of bitter is close to blasphemy. They have avoided that at the Long Boat: the walls are a warm, red brick, related closely to the sort of brick you can see outside, down by the canal; furnishings are solid and don't look as if they'll collapse under your weight. The other feature of a good pub which is so difficult to achieve is the ability to make it big enough for a crowd while keeping a feeling of intimacy where friends can chat. The bar is big, but other parts are split off, so that you can join the general scrum around the bar or retreat into a more private space. Then there is that indefinable thing – character. With old pubs, the character grows up over the years. Here, they have attempted to build a character in. It could have been disastrous, but I think they have succeeded. The bar has a balcony over the canal basin, and the whole pub is made to relate to the canal through decoration and use of canal motifs. The booths, for

The opposite
view of Gas Street, looking towards the stop lock and toll house.

example, are separated by wooden dividers in the form of rudders and stern posts. But the main point in its favour is that it's not a place that turns up its nose at some of the scruffier characters who come in off the boats. It also, incidentally, acts as a sort of answering service for Caggy Stevens, one of the last of the old boatmen still to work horse-drawn boats on the cut. He sends messages through to the crew via the Long Boat telephone, a very handy place to have, seeing that there's usually one or other of his boats tied up outside.

When you start to talk about horse-drawn boats, you can almost feel the waves of nostalgia starting to beat up around you, but a meeting with the Stevens boats soon dispels any notions of a romantic idyll. He mostly shifts rubbish and scrap. The boats are day boats, mucky iron hulls with not a rose or a castle in sight. The horse serves a good practical purpose. Tugs are all right, and he has tugs for the long pounds, but on the heavily locked sections they waste time. You can't fit tug and boat into the lock at the same time. The horse is quicker and cheaper, and that's why it's there. It's not a very good idea, by the way, to describe Caggy Stevens as a romantic figure, at least not while he's in earshot. He's a hardworking man, following a mucky trade, and if anyone chooses to find anything romantic in it, then that's because they haven't been out before dawn on an icy February morning shifting several tons of scrap.

Brummagem is two worlds. There is the world I see from the canal – dirty, often seedy, with a tumbledown, forgotten air to a lot of it, but full of character, independent, a place that has something to say about people and the lives they live. And there's the new Birmingham, the modern city I meet when I leave the cut. For me it's the nightmare realized. And the new Birmingham's winning out, encroaching on the other Birmingham, nibbling away at first, then taking great gobfuls out of it. In the morning I went to see Gas Street Basin, and I could have sat down and wept for what's been lost. When I got home after the trip, I looked up the words I wrote a year before. Here they are, just as I put them down, before I'd even heard there was a threat to the place.

Coming up towards Broad Street and the looming Post Office tower, we came into a wide basin, flanked by old warehouses, their hoists still encased in timber, and a few eighteenth-century cottages and offices. Lined up along wooden walkways are dozens of converted narrow boats. This is Gas Street basin, and the boats are home to the Gas Street locals. It's all a bit shabby. The walkways are alive with dogs that offer a decidedly noisy welcome to trespassers. The traditional painting on many of the boats has that worn air that

speaks of use, not exhibition. Shabby it may be, but I would go down on my knees to preserve it from change. It would be easy to tart it all up, to surround the basin with boutiques and antique markets, repaint the boats and convert them to discos or restaurants. You could advertise the place, open it up as an example of 'local colour'. No one would deny that central Birmingham is sadly in need of local colour, but this just happens to be something more than a show place looking for a 'Come to Britain' silver medal. It is the real thing. People live here and like living here. It's their place, the way they like it. It doesn't bear thinking about what would happen to such a site in London – it would end up as a rich man's ghetto or an office block, like as not. Instead it's just Gas Street, a place with its own character, enclosed, very private in its way.

You have to know Gas Street Basin's there, for you'll never come across it just walking the streets of the city. You walk into Gas Street itself, and there's a gap in a high brick wall. Look through the gap and you see steps leading down behind a second wall. No view, no hint of anything very exciting. But if you know Birmingham canals, you know right away what to expect behind the wall, for set into the brickwork is a wooden hatch, painted bright red. This is a fire point, where firemen can lower their hoses into the water. The sight of one of those hatches is a sure indication of a canal near at hand. But not many people walk down Gas Street, and fewer still go down the steps to explore.

Every city needs its Gas Streets: odd places, different places, not places done up for tourists, but there giving delight to the curious who take the trouble to look for them. It's a touch of humanity, a place that has developed its character from the people who use it, that's happened almost by accident. Try to improve it, plan it and develop it and the whole thing's ruined.

Since writing that, the disaster has happened. The vandals have won, and one whole side of Gas Street Basin has been demolished. The boat community stand as indecently exposed as a nun caught in the shower. In time, they will be closed in again, overlooked by a new office block, which, from the plans, will be an unlovely creature. But no matter what they do, the old air of secrecy has been destroyed, the atmosphere has fled, the irreplaceable has been removed. It is a sad, miserable story. I suppose you could say that the new Gas Street fits better with the new Birmingham image, for it opens out on to the draughty acres of a car park, and it is the motor car that rules in Birmingham.

I do not dislike the motor car. I own a car, use it a good deal, but I do not expect it to take over my life. The car is taking over the life of Birmingham. The motorways loop round the city, then dive into the centre, obliterating the old and driving the wretched pedestrians into a series of rabbity warrens. I once tried to walk from Gas Street to Newhall Street, a distance of half a mile as the crow flies. Lucky crow. I was faced by the inner ring road, which has turned the heart of the city into a lonely island lapped by traffic. The old landmarks have largely gone. The street market has been pushed underground, its space handed over to roads and cars. People have been supplied with 'pedestrian ways', which is officialese for tunnels. The stranger trapped in these tunnels finds he has to keep surfacing to get new directions, and all too often emerges into a sort of no-man's-land, a tiny patch among the busy cars. People were generally very helpful, but for all the success they had they might as well have been trying to conduct me through Hampton Court maze. They say it is all quite simple once you get the hang of it. Maybe so – but that doesn't alter the fact that to penetrate into this city you have long marches through dreary tunnels with only graffiti and adverts to brighten the eye, only the whiff of regurgitated beer to keep the nostrils twitching.

Once you get above ground in Birmingham, there are things to enjoy. I popped up briefly at the unbelievably ill-named Paradise Circus to discover one of the best tall office blocks I have seen in any English city – slender, elegantly curved. The trouble with so many of our new blocks is that they match a dully repetitive facade with a square solidity. They are lumpen. Here shape is all important, and as you look up you sense a lightness, a soaring quality. If we have to build high,

then why cannot we build like this, with a sense of style, using the height to good effect? The only thing wrong here is the site, which is just another fiddly little patch where the rabbit-pedestrians come up for air.

Up and down, up and down: up to ask a direction, down again to try and follow it. After about half an hour, I found I had managed to complete a full circle and had to start all over again. I got there at last, but even when I'd cleared the ring road, there was still one more tunnel to pass. It's all designed to speed the flow of traffic. But aren't the cars ever supposed to stop? Don't motorists ever get out and become pedestrians? Is this really the solution – speed the traffic, speed the traffic, round and round, and leave nowhere for the people? Birmingham at night seemed dead, and no wonder. Who wants a night out on a traffic island?

So I paid my respects to the remains of Gas Street, and was not too sorry to get back to the boat and the fascination of Birmingham's canals. B.C.N., Birmingham Canal Navigations, is a world apart, which I often think you need a lifetime to get to know. Our route was the simplest one, straight down the Birmingham main line -and straight down it is, for this is a late canal, built by Thomas Telford in the 1820s, straight as a rule, proceeding by cutting and embankment with little regard for anything that stood in the way, the nineteenth-century equivalent of the motorway. It is the main stem, from which

Galton Street
Bridge crossing the deep cutting of the Birmingham main line. This view has now been lost, since a lower level road bridge was completed through which the canal passes in a concrete tunnel.

flow a profusion of branches. If the route into Birmingham had something of an industrial character, then the route out is the same but more so. The cut just goes on getting filthier and filthier, changing from a muddy green to a startling indigo. In it and on it float the cast-offs of a city – polystyrene in huge chunks from I know not where, polythene bags in profusion, hair driers and tyres, dead cats and dolls' prams, bedsprings, bathtubs and the head of a cod. Over it all hung a clammy mist, which the billowing clouds of industry could turn into patches of near-impenetrable fog. It is so easy to forget, when we talk of the virtues of industrial growth, that all this is part of the price we have to pay. People live and work among the botched-up factories and mean terraces, breathing the acrid fumes of sulphur, looking out from their front windows at the lowering factory wall. And there are the waste areas, the derelict lands as barren as any desert, the places where man has taken what he wants from the earth, the coal and minerals, and left only devastation behind, great heaps of spoil and flat scrubs. Country doesn't come much blacker than the Black Country.

And yet, and yet, I find myself fascinated by this world, which has so much to offer that is interesting in comparison with the bland sophistication of the city centre. The canal itself offers many delights, and place names make as good a starting point as any. Poets have extolled the virtues of Grasmere and Stoke Poges, but

An unusual example of canal Gothic: Thomas Telford's Engine Arm aqueduct carrying a branch of the canal over the Birmingham main line.

what about Spon Lane and Pudding Green, Wednesbury Oak, Tipton and Bumblehole, Oozells Street Loop and Brasshouse Bridge? Such names deserve their own hymn of praise. The route winds its way through just the strange, rather quirky places such names would lead you to expect.

My favourite structure along the canal is the Engine Arm Aqueduct, a canal flyover, carrying one of the many branches over the main line. It is built of cast-iron, strong and workmanlike, but the builders have turned a purely functional structure into a Gothic fantasy, with rows of pointed arches along the full length of the trough. You could describe it as absurd, but what's so bad about that? In contrast, Galton Street Bridge needs no elaboration to make its presence felt – a majestic span that crosses a deep cutting, a bold, forthright statement in iron. Today it also crosses the canal's newest tunnel, a concrete tube through a road improvement scheme which has taken away something of the visual effect of Galton Bridge. Iron is certainly the most dramatically used material on the canal, and the most graceful, as the many small, simple bridges testify, but some of the great brick bridges, such as Lee Bridge which is built on the skew, are not to be scoffed at either. And even the twentieth century has added its own rather spectacular visual effects to the canal. The motorways, which are such a feature of the Birmingham scene, look decidedly more interesting when seen from underneath than they ever do when seen from on top. The M5, for example, crosses the canal on tall concrete stilts, like a huge colonnade, but for those who want a real motorway wonderland, I recommend a trip down the Birmingham and Fazeley Canal, where it slides through the forest of columns that support the tangle of roads that make up Spaghetti Junction.

Canal travellers often grumble about having to pass through heavily industrialized areas, but I have never been able to understand why. What do they expect? Why do they think the things were built in the first place? And, in any case, there's always a wealth of things to see. It is a constant complaint about British industry that it is behind the times, run-down, antiquated, but, my word, what a visual feast the run-down can provide. Just look at the ingenuity with which people make do and mend. There is one factory in particular where bits have been stuck on here, tacked on there, mostly in corrugated iron, forming a marvellous mixture of colour, shapes and patterns. Just because the whole thing has been done in a quite arbitrary, piecemeal way the grooves in the iron run at different angles, creating a startling Op Art effect. And the colours! Reds, yellows, dirty browns, but somehow, by a piece of luck, they all blend together. Lovely.

Nowadays we tend to frown on unnecessary decoration on industrial buildings. The first industrialists didn't, and the decorated chimneys and classical facades were put there to show the world how proud they were of what they were making. And what they were making was not just Birmingham, but the whole modern world, like it or not. So hats off, as you chug past the Soho works, to the first great Birmingham men, Matthew Boulton and James Watt. It was from here that the steam engines were sent out to power the industrial revolution. There's not a lot to see today. Once it was magnificent, but now there is only just enough left to give a hint of former grandeur. But it does show that industrial success need not mean industrial drabness, and if it need not then it should not.

Wolverhampton, and the descent begins through the Wolverhampton 21 – twenty-one narrow locks that take you down off the Birmingham plateau. At the top level you come to the locks past the roaring furnaces of Bilston steel works and through a lovely, elaborate old bridge, a farewell to the city. These locks never seem hard work, but always amaze. Halfway down, I heard birdsong. At the bottom we reached the Staffs and Worcester Canal, a scene of purely rural peace. Brummagem and the Black Country were suddenly behind us.

The bottom lock on the Wolverhampton flight: the city has been left behind for a more rural setting.

CHAPTER 4

Provincial Pleasures

The transformation from the industrial plateau to the green valley below is complete and startling. You know that the town has to come to an end, but it seems impossible that the end should be that sudden. While you have been puffing and blowing over lock gate and windlass, everything around you has changed, right down to the last, minute detail. Where before you were surrounded by houses and factories, here you are looking out over trees, shrubs and fields. The dark mottled blue of the engineering brick has given way to a rich red, spotted with rusty lichen, and brightened by the green shoots, forcing their way through the cracks in the mortar. Even the water is suddenly clear again. Just a short hop down the Staffs and Worcester, round a sharp bend, and the Black Country is only a memory. We were heading north up the Shropshire Union.

Many canals take their characteristics from the countryside through which they pass. The Oxford Canal, our starting point, fits snugly into the landscape, and the urban canals are creatures of the towns and cities that surround them. The Shropshire Union is different: it makes its own character, and that character has something to do with the land, but a lot more to do with the decisions taken by its chief engineer, Thomas Telford. To understand the special nature of this waterway, you have to go back and delve into its history.

This part of the Shropshire Union began life as the Birmingham and Liverpool Junction Canal, a grand title for an ambitious enterprise. It was built to extend the old Chester Canal down from Nantwich to make a junction with the Staffs and Worcester, and thus provide a through route to Birmingham. The first generation of canals had been built with a wary eye on the landscape. Lumps and bumps on the face of the land were treated with great circumspection, not to mention circumnavigation, so that routes were forced to twist and turn to keep a level. But by the 1820s when this canal was begun, engineering skill had come a long way. If an engineer wanted to take his canal from A to B, then from A to B was where he took it, and damn the landscape. Of course today we would condemn such philistine disregard for natural features, and loudest in condemnation tend to be those – and, alas, I am as guilty as the rest – who are loudest in praise of a route such as the Birmingham and Liverpool Junction Canal.

The technique that Telford used was what is graphically known as 'cut and fill'. If you meet a hill, cut through it, then cart away your spoil to fill up the next valley. So we have a route marked by deep cuttings and high embankments. For those who come this way, it is the narrow artificial gorge that stays in the mind. But for others, the cuttings pass unnoticed, though they are very conscious of the high banks that obliterate the view. They might not, however, be aware that there are boats moving about up there on the top of them. So the canal has wrought a change in the landscape in a way that the older routes never did, and for those who lived through the construction period it must have seemed as if an indelible mark was being inflicted on the land. The cuttings would have been raw wounds in the earth, and the banks heaps of rubble and earth, as lovely as a slag heap. But time has changed all that. The cuts, acting as natural drains for the surrounding land, are as rich in vegetation as any Amazonian rain forest. They seem to be permanently damp, and the sides drip with creepers that climb out over the thick covering of bushes and trees. In high summer it is marvellously, lushly green, almost overpowering in its richness. And the banks, too, have changed: grass has grown, trees have established a hold. Neither bank nor cut could ever be mistaken as anything but an unnatural intrusion in the land, but at least they now make a positive contribution, add something new, don't merely subtract from the countryside.

The elegant bridge at Atherley Junction, looking up the Shropshire Union Canal.

None of this spectacular scenery puts in an appearance during the first few miles. Indeed, you could say that the beginning is as un-spectacular as any beginning can be. After plunging down the Wolverhampton flight, you now face a lock that will take you down in a rather less impressive drop of six inches. The lock only ever had one function in life, and even that function no longer has any relevance. In the old days of independent companies, the canal owners were jealous guardians of their most valuable possession - water. The Shropshire Union runs downhill from the junction, so the Staffs and Worcester Company insisted on the lock being built to act as a dam. The new company could get out and find their own water. They did and do. Water for this section – unsavoury thought – comes from the nearby sewage works. In dry days like those we were seeing, the cry can be heard going up from the Shroppie – keep peeing, Birmingham!

A gentle run but what pleasures it offers. My heart leaps up when I behold – well, in my case, stone bridges. To see well dressed stones bonding together to form the arch of a bridge always seems to me a glimpse of the miraculous. Even now, when I know how it's done, understand the principle of the thing, the arch still seems to be one of man's boldest inventions. And there are so many skills involved – the skill of the quarryman who selects and cuts the stone, the skill of the mason who shapes the blocks, the skill of the builder. Even the plainest stone bridges are a delight, but occasionally you also get something rather special. Just before Brewood, the canal passes through the park of Chillington Hall, and here the unnatural canal meets an unnatural landscape. This was the work of Capability Brown, who is probably the first gardener since Adam to achieve lasting fame. His blend of the natural and artificial, his reordering of the countryside to suit his own ideal of beauty, helped to make the English landscape garden into a work of art. When you see one of his great works, you can understand the enthusiasm behind this tribute from an anonymous poet of the eighteenth century.

He barren tracts with every charm illumes,
At his command a new Creation blooms;
Born to grace Nature, and her works complete,
With all that's beautiful, sublime and great:
   For him each Muse unwreathes the Laurel Crown,
   And consecrates to Fame immortal Brown.

Canals might not seem to have very much to do with that sort of sentiment, but the builders rose to the challenge of Brown's park by providing an elegantly balustraded bridge, altogether much grander than the common arch you find everywhere else. Of course, they didn't have a lot of choice in the matter. The big landowner was a powerful force in those days, and unless you wanted a detour or a lengthy legal wrangle you would probably lose, then you did your best to placate. An elegant bridge probably seemed a very modest price to pay.

We stopped for the night at Brewood. If you look for the place on the map, you find that it's not much more than a dot in a tangle of minor roads, just beyond the edge of the creeping suburbs of Wolverhampton. It is just one of those myriad places that are there for no apparent reason, and seem to offer few obvious attractions to lure the hurrying motorist from his travels. If you look at a larger scale map, though, some interesting facts start to emerge. First Brewood is on a hilltop – the name originally meant Wood on the Hill – so it was one of the obvious places for an early settlement. Look next to the north, and you see that unmistakable straight line that marks the Roman Road – Watling Street, emerging from the dark forests of Cannock Chase. You would expect a hill overlooking the road to prove very attractive to the Romans and, sure enough, the site of a Roman villa is marked on the map. Brewood was established, and grew up as a small centre, serving the surrounding countryside.

Brewood, then, has a long history, but that in itself might not seem much of a reason to stop there. Certainly, the canal traveller could slip through the place and scarcely register its presence, for the engineers treated Brewood Hill with scant respect, slicing through the middle, leaving the town divided by a chasm. All you can see from down on the water are the two churches, poking over the horizon, Catholic on one side of the cut, Protestant on the other. In fact, we stopped there for no better reason than that we had had a long day and the next likely stopping place was a bit too far away. But, having stopped, I soon discovered what a good choice it was. I have travelled this way before, and have long appreciated the character of the canal, but this was the first time I had taken a really good look at any of the villages and towns, large and small, along the way.

The village may have a long history, but its appeal today owes almost everything to the Georgians. There is an air of unassuming prosperity about the place, and how well Georgian architecture fits into such a mood. It evokes feelings of calm and good order, of life organized in a reasonable way for men of sound reason. Those careful, exact proportions of the Georgian facade, the porticoed door, flanked by tall windows, the rather smaller windows on the upper floor, providing a

The year the trip was taken, England had been suffering from a severe drought: there was not much sign of it on the journey along the Shropshire Union, hence the author's rather glum expression.

sense of regularity without the least sense of dullness: it all seems to speak of a world in which everything runs to the same well ordered rules. Yet while the prosperous gentlemen of Georgian Brewood were building their new houses, the world was being revolutionized, and the revolution was coming right up to their clean, new doorsteps. Down in the cutting, the navvies were there in their thousands, sweating over pick and spade to bring the new technology to this apparently timeless calm. Just as there is more to the Georgian age than the quiet dignity of the old houses, so too there is something a bit odd about the houses themselves. Look closely at some of those Brewood houses, and look especially at those fine tall windows – some of them turn out not to be windows at all but simply paint on brick, a strange phenomenon with a simple explanation. The culprit was the window tax, surely one of the silliest taxes of all times. House owners resorted to the paint-brush rather than foot the bill or destroy that essential symmetry.

The Georgian housing may dominate the main streets, but there are still a few reminders that not everyone lived so grandly. Next to the garage, squashed now into a narrow confine, is a much older half-timbered cottage of the sort that must have been common here before the eighteenth-century mania for improvement and modernization got under way. Were there conservationists around then, desperately defending wattle and daub and thatch against the newfangled brick and tile? Georgian houses, timbered cottages – how very fortunate we are that we can just accept these as part of an ordinary small town in provincial England. But even the ordinary small town has its one surprise. There in the very centre is a masterpiece of Gothic elaboration, a building in which every window and door is topped by a grotesque ogee arch, a final touch of eccentricity to add to an already rich mixture. And at the end of the day, bell practice, proper bell practice. There was none of that foreign nonsense about playing tunes. This was change ringing, an art that owes more to mathematics than to music, and one which, as anyone who lives as I do within earshot of a belfry can testify, requires long and, to the untrained ear, painful practice.

Shortly after you leave Brewood on the canal you come to a spot where Telford, the engineer, went in for a little justifiable self-congratulation. Near Stretton, the canal crosses the main Holyhead Road on a short cast-iron aqueduct. The engineering of the road was also the work of Mr Telford, and the conjunction of Telford canal crossing Telford road could not be allowed to pass without comment. Just a little bit extra was allowed in the way of embellishment: pleasant

Deep cuttings
are a striking
feature of the
Shropshire Union,
many crossed by
high bridges such
as this.

rounded stone pillars mark the ends, the trough is now smart in fresh black and white paint, and those who care to look up from the road will find the inscription where Telford set out the record of his deeds.

This was the day when we really met the cuttings and banks. The cuts are crossed by high bridges, known from the tapering of the arch as rocket bridges, which are much admired but when I get down in those cuts I am always most conscious of the great effort of the men who dug the canals in the days before mechanical excavators were in use. These cuts are all about muscle power and brawn and the long, frightening climbs up the barrow runs. Up the steep, slippery planks the navvies went, their barrow loads of spoil balanced in front of them, while somewhere out of sight a horse took the strain of the load. How many men slipped and fell, the barrow, soil and rock cascading around them, over them? Go down Grub Street cut or Woodseaves and think to yourself of the sweat and the effort that went into their making. How many millions of cubic feet of earth were shifted? And it was not just muck either; solid rock had to be moved as well. Cowley tunnel is only eighty yards long, but it was rough-hewn from the rock, just as the cutting beyond it was hacked out of the stone. Your boat slides past tall rock walls that still bear the marks of pick and drill, the only signatures the men of that great anonymous army left to posterity.

Out of the cutting and up on the bank – what comes out of the holes fills in the gaps. If the cuts were the navvies' nightmare, then the banks sent many an engineer white-haired to an early grave. Shelmore Great Bank was the biggest and the most troublesome. Every time they built it up, it slipped. The engineers were like the Grand Old Duke of York. They were continuously marching their ten thousand men up to the top of the hill, only to have to march them down again. What must have made the whole thing especially galling to Telford was that he never wanted to put the canal there in the first place. It was the local nobs at Knightley Hall who wanted the canal kept well clear of their back doors, thank you very much. They weren't even interested in acquiring an ornamental bridge. So the great bank was built, but Telford was dead before it was finally opened in 1835. Even then it was only wide enough, at first, to take one-way traffic. When you come up to the bank, you can still see the gates set at the end, ready to close off the section if it should ever collapse again.

All the way north from Brewood, we were able to take life easy: nearly twenty-five miles of canal, and not a lock in sight. There was time to look around and enjoy the countryside, already freshening with the first green touches of Spring. This is a rich land of grazing cattle and scattered farms, of wide spaces and long horizons. We had time, too, to renew acquaintance with a few favourite canalside places. There was the Boat Inn at Gnosall, an odd-shaped building, which has one wall curved around to fit an awkward angle between the bridge and the canal. Then there were the neat, spick-and-span workshops at Norbury, with the old forge and a general air of belonging to an older world of crafts rather than to modern industry. And when we had to stop staring and start working, the locks brought their own special pleasure.

Tyrley locks are, like most of the locks on this canal, closely grouped, which makes for easy working. They are also like the others in that they are beautifully maintained and a credit to the lock keeper. You arrive at the top to find a pleasantly open setting, the canal flanked by an old warehouse and cottages, built in 1837, just after the opening of the canal. Sadly these are in a state of dilapidation, and it is depressing because they are fine buildings that deserve a better fate. As you leave them behind and start down the locks, the ground begins to close in on either side and when you reach the bottom you are quite hemmed into a little cutting with steep sandstone sides, as dark and enclosed as a cave in the woods. It is a lovely contrast to be savoured. There was also a reassuring rumble from the water that poured over the weir, promising that water shortage was not going to be an immediate problem.

We moored at Market Drayton. It was bell night. We seemed to be following a special campanologist's tour. Brewood gives you some sort of idea of just how much pleasure can be found in an ordinary village; Market Drayton does the same for the market town, though nowadays Market Drayton has lost some of its former importance. Market towns no longer have quite the same vital role to play in the national economy, which is one mark of how we have moved from being an agricultural to an industrial nation. But it was important once all right, and that importance is reflected in a wealth of good building. The virtue of such a place doesn't stem from the possession of some one, very grand building: there are no grandiose gestures here. Rather there is the pleasure to be gained from an accumulation of small things. I don't suppose anyone is going to put Market Drayton on the tourist map as an essential, not-to-be-missed-at-any-cost sort of place. But if you want to feel something of the small provincial centre, then this is as good a place to come as any.

There is a certain coherence about Market Drayton which is, quite literally, accidental for the whole town was burned down in the

The only "double bridge" on the Shropshire Union.

middle of the seventeenth century. A few of the old black and white buildings which are so typical of the region do still stand – Sandbrook Vaults and the National Westminster Bank are the best examples. This sort of building is much admired often, I think, because people have a sort of feeling that anything that old has to be admirable. I'd feel more warmth towards them if the exposed timbers had been left as natural wood, and not blacked over. The trouble is that the whole style has been so horribly debased in the present century: all those acres of Home Counties mock-Tudor have done for the real thing. The originals tend to look like mock-Tudor, too – only seedier. Half the time you don't even register that they are the real thing at all; the eye just takes in the form of the stockbroker's mansion and flicks on to something else. Too much imitation inevitably reduces the original.

The one inescapable, dominant feature in the town is the church, which stands lofty on its eminence over the Tern valley. It has a fine fourteenth-century tower, though the rest has suffered from the heavy-handed restoration of the Victorian ecclesiastical *Blitzkreig*. Still, that doesn't matter too much for it is the tower that is visible – and, on bell night, audible – everywhere, while the rest of the church appears in glimpsed snatches through the complicated street pattern of the town. How good to find somewhere that offers such a bewildering pattern, such a mixture of views, down wide streets and narrow alleys, up steps and over the crest of the hill. This is the greatest single blessing that results from the slow growth of a town.

Market Drayton tends to keep the canal at arm's length but down by the wharf fine warehouses, as fine in their own way as the town centre, provide ample evidence of the old trading and commercial prosperity. I am especially fond of the Farmers' Warehouse, a great wedge of a building, strongly reminiscent of the cheeses it must often have housed – ah! for the halcyon days when Cheshire cheese came from Cheshire, and Cheddar was still more suitable for the table than the bathroom. Not that we had much chance to enjoy the shape of the building or anything else when we set out the next morning. The mist had come down in the night and the whole world was vague and indistinct. The warehouses loomed out of the fog like a set for *The Flying Dutchman*. All morning that mist lingered. The sun, tantalizingly, kept appearing as a pallid disc. Aha, you thought, the sun's out, the mist will soon shift – but down came the gloom again. The brief appearances of the sun gave little light and less warmth. Steering became a difficulty. In a long boat you tend to steer towards points some way ahead of the bows. You can't do that in the mist, so bends and turns come up on you

The boat emerging from Cowley tunnel on the Shropshire Union.

unawares, and instead of moving in a steady, smooth curve, you shove the boat about in a series of sharp, jerky movements.

Adderley locks and Audlem locks, which if nothing else gave us a chance to warm up a bit, and as we went down the Audlem flight, down past the sentinel firs and telegraph poles that mark the route, the sun finally decided to put in an appearance. We said thank you very much and promptly left it to get on with it as we disappeared into the canal's newest pub, the Shroppie Fly. This used to be a warehouse and outside the old cast-iron casement windows still give a strong hint of its origin. Sadly, the warm red brick has been covered over. Inside, the pub teeters on the edge of tweedom, with a bar constructed out of half a narrow boat, and canal prints on the wall. Fortunately, the prints are good and genuinely interesting, the bar-boat is authentic, and we have been spared a profusion of roses and castles. There is a certain air of solidity about the place, and it really is good to see these buildings, which contribute so much to the atmosphere of the canal, being put to use again.

Suitably refreshed, we came out to find that the sun was still shining, and we made our way via a long sweeping bank and a short aqueduct to Nantwich, where we were joined by Mike Ware who was to keep us company for the next two weeks. Mike is a paragon of unflappability. If there was an announcement on the radio that the world was ending at three that afternoon, Mike would light his pipe and wander off to finish his Scotch to make sure it wasn't wasted.

Nantwich is another place that the canal never quite reaches. I have been there a number of times, but either laziness or the need to hurry on to somewhere else have kept me from making that short walk into town. But now, with the experience of Brewood and Market Drayton behind me, I felt rather keen to try one more town before we changed direction and moved off to another part of the country. And, as though to remind me that this was indeed a place that followed tradition, bell practice started up right on cue.

The citizens of this part of the world seem to have been rather careless with their matches. Nantwich, like Market Drayton, was also destroyed by fire but slightly earlier, in 1583, and as a plaque in the town informs you, Queen Elizabeth helped pay for the rebuilding. For Nantwich was a very important place, and the 'wich' part of the name tells you why. It was one of the great centres of salt production and the salt trade, and it was on salt that the town's prosperity was built. Not that that represented the end of the town's story, and a walk into the centre gives you as good a history lesson as any learned article. Here you can find a progress chart of the town's development.

Walking down the main road in from the north, the most obvious point of interest is a group of nineteenth-century alms houses. Fine enough in their way, but look across the road at the little group of

The former wharf building at Audlem has been converted into the "Shroppie Fly" pub.

eighteenth-century cottages, masterpieces of make-do ingenuity, slotting into any available space. Mostly they are two-storey, but where one gap proved particularly small, the builder managed to squeeze in an absurdly narrow house, then pushed it up to a third story by way of compensation. It was while I was walking past this row that another house caught my eye. A workman's cottage, yes – but what were those large windows on the upper floor? No workman ever went to that sort of expense just for living-room light, not in an age when the wealthy burghers of Brewood were painting artificial windows on their houses. No, that was quite definitely a workshop window. Somebody must have been making something in the home. It couldn't be anything to do with salt, so what was it? The mystery is not too difficult to solve if you keep an eye open for street names. Mill Street – now that has a promising sound to it, and if you walk down Mill Street, you find the mill, an absolutely unmistakable, small, late-eighteenth-century cotton mill. So now you know that textiles came to Nantwich, and those big windows were weavers' windows, casting light on to the old hand loom. Another layer of history has been revealed. I have often thought it would be an interesting exercise to visit some town about which I knew nothing whatsoever, and see how much I could discover of its past just by walking and observing.

Nantwich is a town where you hop from period to period all the time. The Tudor rebuilding gives an idea of how important the place was, even if you don't know about the royal patronage. There is a wealth of these early buildings, often very imposing and grand, and they are all mixed up with some equally grand and imposing Georgian ones. In fact, leading out from the market square is a Georgian terrace as splendid as anything you'd find in Hampstead or Bath, and opposite that, tucked away down a dark alley, without so much as a sign to announce its presence, is the Bowling Green. This was just the sort of pub that locals know and tend, very sensibly, not to tell anyone else about. However, one of the locals we met on our walk round the town mentioned the place which he described as 'pretty basic'. He was right: basic is just what it is – a snug little bar with real ale and pleasant company. There are no refinements, no frills, but who needs them when the basics are right? I almost felt I was back in my own local, and you can't say fairer than that.

Like all the best pubs, the place owes a lot of its character to its landlord, a spry, upright gentleman with a magnificent white beard. He is much given to singing – no special tune, no concert performance, just sudden, rather startling outbursts when the mood takes him. He also has a curious, rather Dickensian style of speech, in which his ale is always 'bitter beer' and never just your ordinary 'bitter'. They say the big breweries are moving back to the system of bringing in landlords instead of the managers they have favoured of late. And about time too. The good landlord can stamp his personality on the pub, for he knows he might be spending the best part of his working life there. The manager wants to 'maximize profits' in the economists' favourite phrase. In practice, and you can see it in pubs up and down the country, this means removal of the public bar and, of course, the scruffs who went with it, and a 'new image' to attract new customers. The dart board goes out and the scampi and chips come in. It often works for a while, until the novelty wears off. Then the new customers fade away and the old customers stay away. And the manager? If he's timed it right he's already moved on to a bigger and better place.

I spent a good part of the evening at the Bowling Green chatting to the barman, a native of Nantwich and a lover of his native town, anxious to see its character preserved. He also turned out to be a fund of esoteric information. I've always said working in a pub was a great education, but it was only then that I discovered that a good part of that education can come from reading the backs of crisp packets. It was all reminiscent of the barman in Eric Linklater's *Poet's Pub* who gleaned his knowledge from cigarette cards. At the end of the evening the barman begged us to go and see the new National Westminster Bank which had replaced an old Georgian building. So I did, but I really

This photograph of the bottom lock at Tyrley was taken at a later date: it is a reminder that in good weather the Shropshire Union is a remarkably attractive waterway.

cannot join in his cries of woe. What I found was an unashamedly modern building, built from the new materials of glass, concrete and steel, but using them with a sense of style and, most importantly, with an awareness of what was going on around it. It kept the levels and proportions of the street, and fitted in with the Georgian as well as the Georgian in its day had fitted the Tudor.

You can so easily see what has gone right and what has gone wrong when you stand in the centre of a town like Nantwich. At first glance you see a succession of shop fronts all but identical in their plate glass anonymity and multiple-store standardized image. But lift your eyes above ground-floor level, and what a wealth of interest, what variety there is to be seen. This is one of the great secrets of the country, the not-quite-hidden, rich diversity of the unassuming provincial town.

CHAPTER 5

Mills and Hills

Nantwich was decision time: either we were to go north on the Trent and Mersey and up to the Bridgewater Canal and Manchester, or we would be able to take the less direct but more interesting route via the Macclesfield and Peak Forest Canals. It all depended on a mile and a half of waterway which, due to a historical accident, had remained in private ownership. Was the Rochdale Canal open through Manchester? A phone call produced the information that it was, indeed, open for navigation. But – there always seems to be a 'but' in these situations – there were bureaucratic problems to be overcome. When I had first enquired some weeks before, the Rochdale Canal Company had offered to sell me a licence, although they said they were quite certain I should not be able to use it. I had politely declined that untempting offer. Now, with no licence, I was told to keep away, and, no, they would not sell me a licence when I got there. Eventually they accepted my lengthy arguments, and allowed me to send a cheque in advance. The route was decided.

Above Nantwich, there is a short haul up to Barbridge Junction, where we cut off to the east along the ten miles of the Middlewich Branch. I suppose this length of canal ought to have a special nostalgic place in my affections as the first length of canal I ever travelled, but somehow I have never been able to take it seriously. It is simply not a real canal in its own right, just a connection between two other major routes. It doesn't even boast a proper name - just plain Middlewich Branch. Compare that with the two routes it joins, which luxuriate in two names apiece – the Liverpool and Birmingham or Shropshire Union at one end and the Trent and Mersey or Grand Trunk at the other – and you can see how easily an inferiority complex could develop. When this nameless insignificance is added to a bitterly cold day, one could not blame the traveller for showing more interest in a warm cabin than an icy landscape. All of which is a pity, because there is something about the Middlewich Branch that makes it more than a mere conjunction.

The branch is so straight and true that it needs no expert eye to distinguish it as belonging to the later age of canal building. There are no towns, no villages even, on its banks, but the banks themselves are often high enough to give grand, panoramic views of the surrounding country. They also give a clear enough view of little villages such as Church Minshull to make you wish your route took you closer. You pass above an area where the river Weaver meets a number of small lakes, which seem strange and out of place in a predominantly flat landscape. Natural lakes occur in folds and hollows in the ground, and there is a sense of balance as the earth rises up around the depression. But here the earth has simply collapsed in on itself. Beneath the lakes, men once burrowed and dug in the mines, and when they were gone the collapse came. And these mining flashes are the result.

At Middlewich itself- another of the salt 'wiches' – we joined the Trent and Mersey, off the motorway and on to the country lanes, as it were. This has always been a great favourite of mine, largely because of its historical associations. It was the first, major through route to be started, hence the fine, important name of Grand Trunk, and its chief promoter was a gentleman for whom I have developed a certain affection over the years, Mr Josiah Wedgwood. But for all that, it can be an irritating route to travel. Brindley, the engineer, was very inclined to stagger his locks out along the route. They always seem to be so far apart that walking becomes a chore, but then if you opt for laziness and get back on the boat you scarcely have rime to make yourself

Having left the Shropshire Union via the Middlewich Branch, the journey has arrived at this attractive bridge by the Kings Lock pub.

comfortable before you are up and off again. It is all rather frustrating, but the frustration is greatly eased by finding so much of interest to see along the way.

Turning south at Middlewich junction, you don't quite get to see the town: what you do see is the industry that lines the road and keeps you company. There are still salt works here, though, as with all factories concerned with foodstuff, it is never a good idea to look too closely – not that there is the least suspicion that the works are run to anything but the very highest standards, but it all does look so desperately unappetizing. Salt here has none of the purity of the homely salt cellar: it cascades to the floor in a dull grey avalanche. It reminded me of a visit I once paid to a food-processing plant where men were literally shovelling spaghetti into a huge machine. No, in these cases, ignorance is definitely more blissful than knowledge. Around Etley Heath, the mining flashes can again be seen next to the canal. By now they are integrated so thoroughly with the landscape that they have become a sort of semi-industrial, semi-rural feature, and you get the mixture echoed in local names such as Crabtree Flash Mill. We passed close to an abandoned salt works, timbers falling into the grimy salt that lay thick on the floor. It was a last view of Cheshire's little Siberia.

The canal swings away from the road and away from industry: hedges disappear and the green fields creep up to the water's edge. Hillocks rise and each side of the canal is bounded by springy turf, grazed by disinterested sheep. There is a marvellous open feeling about it all. Normally a canal will be open on one side, but on the towpath side it will be carefully screened, marked off by a hedge or wall. It is this which tends to give the canal the air of secrecy, of being part of a rather private landscape. But not here, and how unobtrusively, how naturally it fits into the scene. The same cannot be said of the railways. The canals bequeathed their new technology to the railways, and the railways went on from there. Where the canal engineers developed the technique of cut and fill, the railway engineers dug deeper cuts, built greater banks. Here the bank is plonked down, a straight life ruled on the land which could never be mistaken for a natural feature, and electrification has emphasized its artificiality. The gantries are a regiment, parading out to the horizon in seemingly endless repetition.

Yet even the railway, so modern in comparison with our wandering watery route, is threatened with obsolescence. The rate of change began to accelerate with the canal age, but even the most ardent advocates of modernization in that time could not have prophesied that it would go on and on gathering speed. Yesterday's technology now passes into a sort of instant nostalgia: the locomotives take over from the canal boats, and we turn to the canals for pleasure; the diesel locomotive replaces the steam, and steam societies pop up on the instant. How long to 'Preserve the Diesel[5] or 'Keep the Electrics', or even 'Reopen the MI? And now, just as I write these words, the latest and likeliest candidate for the technological scrapyard passes overhead, a beautiful, but sadly absurd machine – Concorde.

We moored for the night at Rode Heath, a hybrid sort of place. Down by the canal, you can see the Rode Heath mixture in miniature. Two locks stand side by side: on one side is the familiar narrow lock, hardly changed in its essentials in the last two centuries. Beside it is the extraordinary metal box known as Thurlwood steel lock, painted elephant grey, though elephant white would be more appropriate. The steel lock was put there in 1957 to combat subsidence. It was successful, so successful that it held up the old lock, which is still used, unlike the steel lock, an edifice that manages to combine maximum ugliness with minimum practicality. The old and the new sit uneasily together, and the same can be said of Rode Heath.

The canal shows you the best of Rode Heath; it shows you, in fact, the features that have made Rode Heath popular. Here are the old cottages, not startlingly beautiful, but unpretentious, homely places, at ease with their surroundings. Here, too, is a fine and majestic mill, built out over the canal so that boats could slip in under the archway to load up, safe from the vagaries of the weather. This, you tend to feel, is how things always used to be. But you would be wrong. What we are looking at is the Rode Heath of the post-canal age. Brick walls, slate roofs – these are not in the old tradition of the area. Brick was scarcely known hereabouts until the late eighteenth century. Over in nearby Burslem, there was a house known simply as The Brick House, and that was quite enough to distinguish it from all its neighbours. And slate – slate was quite unknown. Thomas Pennant, writing in 1782, enthused over the changes made possible by the opening of the new canal: 'The cottage, instead of being half-covered with miserable thatch, is now secured with a substantial covering of tiles or slate, brought from the distant hills of Wales or Cumberland.' So the wheel turns, and the miserable thatch that once covered the homes of the poor is now prized by the wealthy.

Change has come to Rode Heath, and it is one of those places where the coming of change now seems inevitable. It is close to Stoke, full of character – just the sort of jampot to attract waspish developers. So the new estates have come, and they have no relationship with the old.

Double locks on the Trent & Mersey on the approach to the junction with the Macclesfield Canal.

There is no sense that the builders recognize that old Rode Heath had a distinctive character of its own which was worth preserving. The houses are not bad houses in themselves, far from it, but they have nothing at all to do with Rode Heath as it existed before they came. New Rode Heath and old Rode Heath are like the two Thurlwood locks, side by side but totally unconnected.

We set off next day in morning sunshine. The wind was cold, but the sight of the sun was a great compensation. As you climb the hill towards Kidsgrove and the start of the Potteries the canal turns from its normal, muddy self to a startling orangey-brown, remarkably like tomato soup. It was here that we swung back north. At Harding's Wood, the Macclesfield Canal turns off at an acute angle and runs parallel to the Trent and Mersey, before turning again to go over the Red Bull locks – a canal flyover.

The Macclesfield Canal. Some names are exotic, others merely prosaic, and Macclesfield comes very much in the latter category. It is something to do with that hard, northern 'a' at the beginning of the word. 'Macclesfield': the word comes from the lips as flat as a Yorkshire pudding that's failed to rise, which all goes to show that names can be thoroughly and completely misleading, for there are few more pleasant, exciting or, if it comes to that, romantic routes to travel than the Macclesfield Canal. What, indeed, could be more picturesque than the view to the east, where the hill of Mow Cop rises up, topped by a ruined castle? How perfectly the ruins are shaped; how well the outline fits the smoothly rounded hill. So it should, for it was designed to fit in the first place. The 'castle' is an eighteenth-century folly, a whimsical piece of ruin building, that delights most people and offends only the most rigid of purists. What, I wonder, would be the chances of anyone building a folly, today? Can you imagine going to the local planning office for permission to construct a ruin?

You have a little time to take in the pleasant sight of Mow Cop on your right hand, before the even greater attraction of the Bird-in-Hand at Kent Green beckons on the other. There used to be a lot of pubs like this at one time, but there are precious few of them left. The uninitiated could be forgiven for thinking he had blundered into someone's living room: no bar in sight, just a couple of men sat at their ease by the fireside, while the lady of the house leans at her kitchen door. No beer handles, no bottles, no glasses. But just ask for your beer and the good lady trots off down the cellar steps to tap one of the wooden barrels, and comes back with as good a pint as you'll ever taste. An awful lot of nonsense is written about real ale these days, based on the curious notion that any beer that is hand-pumped or, better still, drawn from the wood, must, by definition, be superb. What rubbish! In the days before keg beers were introduced no one would have convinced me that every beer was worth drinking. But when it is good, and it doesn't come much better than at Kent Green, there's nothing to touch real ale. There's a genuine flavour there to be savoured, and you're not filled up with gas before you're halfway down the pint.

Everything you see along the Macclesfield tells you that you are moving away from the Midlands and on towards the north. The Pennine hills rise up to one side, flanking the canal. From Mow Cop onwards, the skyline takes on that special Pennine quality. These hills are often called the backbone of England, and how apt the name is, for it is here that the hard bones of the land show through. At the tops, the dark rock penetrates the thin veneer of soil and turf making a hard edge to the land. There is little enough comfort in this landscape; there is instead a sense of the elemental strengths of wind and weather. The rocks stand, but the years have worked on them and the scree slopes tongue down below the crags, shattered rocks sliding down the hillside. As the clouds pile over those tops, ragged edges threatening rain, there is a sense of great exhilaration at being part of a land that has stayed unconfined, aloof from the careful markings and scratchings with which man tries to order the world to his own ends.

The route, though, stays well down below these peaks, and over to the west there is the gentler landscape of the valleys where man has dominated and ordered the natural world. Here is Ramsdell Hall, the very opposite of the crude roughness of the hills. Here where everything seems to be a model of elegant sophistication, civilization reigns. The house itself was built in the 1760s, with a regular facade dominated by Venetian windows that look out over smooth lawns that come down to the water's edge. Back door scenery this may be, but what a back door. Two centuries ago Thomas Bentley wrote a pamphlet in which he tried to convince the landowners and aristocrats of the many virtues of canals. 'And here it must be observed and allowed,' he wrote, 'that to have a lawn terminated by water, with objects passing and repassing upon it, is a finishing of all others the most desirable. And if we add the amusements of a pleasure-boat that may enable us to change the prospect, imagination can scarcely conceive the charming variety of such a landscape.' Ramsdell Hall and the Macclesfield Canal together provide conclusive proof of the truth of Bentley's words. Not so very far away, and just visible in the valley, is that most famous of black and white buildings, Little Moreton Hall. It is a riot of patterns, and has an apparent tendency to lean simultaneously in every direction which gives it an air of desperate instability. It is vivid, giddy, mildly nonsensical and wholly strange. And if the canal never offers sight of anything quite that strange again, it does at least keep managing to turn up its surprises.

At Hall Green where the Trent & Mersey joins the Macclesfield Canal, the water has turned a reddish-brown, stained by ochre.

Starting with a folly and continuing on past Little Moreton Hall, how could it ever settle down to the merely mundane?

The character of the canal is derived mainly from these rocky Pennine hills, for it is stone that marks the route and gives it its special quality. This is a very late canal, so late, in fact, that it nearly wasn't a canal at all. The planners were undecided whether to build a waterway or take a chance on one of those new-fangled railways. Being late, it displays all the confidence that the engineers had built up over the years. Here are the high banks, the deep cuts, the grouped locks, but even without these obvious signs, one can sense that self-confidence of the builders in the strength and solidity of all the structures one meets. These were not built to satisfy some temporary need: they have the look of permanence about them. The bridges are masterpieces of the mason's art, not because they are brilliantly carved or extravagantly ornate, but because they are perfect for the job. The most famous examples are the 'snake' bridges, designed to take the towpath from one side of the canal to the other without the need for the boatman to unhitch his horse. The towpath comes in under the arch then curls right round on itself to cross the bridge and go on down the other side. The line of the parapet describes a lovely, sinuous spiral: it is graceful of line, and elegant as a solution to a particular practical problem.

Beyond Congleton, the hilly nature of the land becomes more pronounced. Now it is the massive bulk of The Cloud that dominates the land to the north, while the canal itself sits up high on a bank with magnificent views out over the valley, Here, too, is a timely reminder that it was not just canal engineers who could build structures that combined grace and strength. The aqueduct which crosses the river Dane is handsome enough in its way, but it can't begin to compete with the railway viaduct that marches across the valley, taking the river easily in its stride. But the canal recovers quickly as we come to the one flight of locks on the canal, the Bosley locks, which follow the curve of the hill and hft you over a hundred feet in a dozen watery steps. There are just the right number here: not enough to make you feel you have a slog to get up them, but enough to warm you up on a cold afternoon. The result is a perfect combination, self-satisfaction without undue exertion. All that was left after that was a gentle dawdle along, twisting past woods and hills to a mooring at Oakgrove.

Spring arrived the next day – officially, that is. The calendar certainly presented the information with no hints of doubt or suggestion of error. Unfortunately, those in charge of such matters either failed to read the calendar or were possessed of a nasty, vicious sense of humour.

For spring came in to the accompaniment of rain, hail and sleet. So what had happened to all that blue sky and perpetual sunshine of the brochures? Ah well, if nothing else, a day like that provided a useful corrective to the sentimental image of the old days on the canal. How many winter days far worse than this did the old boatmen know? They had no nice, centrally-heated cabin to retire to while someone else took a turn at the tiller. And there was no question of calling it a day if the weather proved too much. There was a living to be earned. We play at canal travel, but we don't know the half of it.

We passed a pair of swans. It was a common enough occurrence but either the rain was getting them down or we had arrived at some crucial point in the spring courtship. Whatever the reason the male swan took offence. Head tucked down deep into his wings for streamlining, he set off in pursuit of the boat. At first he looked rather comical, like a pompous Victorian burgher in high, white collar. The impression vanished as he came closer. There is nothing very amusing about an angry swan. The bird suddenly seemed very large, very menacing. The water churning out from the prop seemed to annoy him greatly, and he began pecking viciously at the stern of the boat, his neck curling back on itself then shooting out like a coiled spring. When that had no effect he decided to frighten the boat to death.

The most striking features on the Macclesfield Canal are the "turnover" or "snake" bridges, that enable a horse towing a boat to cross the canal without being unhitched.

He reared up on the water, wings outstretched, flailing wildly. Phil had the misfortune to be steering at the time and all this ferocious activity was taking place inches away from his unprotected ankles. You hear stories of people suffering broken arms and legs after attacks by swans, and those stories suddenly seemed very credible. The swan might not have known it, but though he was not frightening the boat, he was terrifying Phil.

We decided that our only hope lay in bribery, so we cast our bread upon the water. It seemed to work. The swan stopped its angry threshing and paused for the snack. Our self-congratulation, however, proved to be premature. Once the bread was gone, the swan was back again at the pursuit. But where before he had been happy enough just to swim after us, now he headed for the boat like a mad thing. Wings beat the air, feet slapped down on the surface of the water and the neck snaked forwards as though the creature could scarcely wait to get at us. Cravenly we sacrificed yet more of our one and only loaf, and in the end the bird got through the best part of it before he finally abandoned the pursuit. It seemed a small price to pay.

You reach Macclesfield, only to discover that the town is all but invisible, for the canal dives into a deep cutting, and for most of the way the only view you have is of the high stone wall that borders the cut. You do, however, make a few forays into the open, enough to get an idea of the industrial background, with glimpses of the old silk weavers' cottages, for it was on silk that the town's prosperity was built. Even then, it's little more than a hint at a busy history, until industry really does arrive with a bang and Hovis Mill looms into view, impressive rather than beautiful; bold, powerful but graceless. The facade is marked by row upon row of plain windows, square and unadorned, and the only relief to this regularity comes with the archway under which boats once passed. It is a great pity you don't see more of Macclesfield but with cut and fill it is all rather like tossing a coin: if it comes up 'cut' you see nothing but high walls, and if it comes up 'fill' you are in for a bird's-eye view. The next town, Bollington, comes up fill.

The approach to Bollington is dramatic. Before you reach the town itself, you come up to Adelphi Mill, as fantastic as the Hovis Mill is plain. It doesn't look too odd at first glance. There is the same regular pattern of windows – and then you notice the tower at the end. The prosaic will tell you that it is simply a water tower, but up it sticks, tipped with fantastic pinnacles in the very best fairy-tale tradition. It was all quiet when we went past. They were probably asleep in there, hundreds of spellbound textile workers waiting for Prince Charming's kiss.

Where the canal meets a main road at Marple at the start of the Peak Forest Canal, horses have been provided with their very own tunnel under the road.

You come past the mill and over two aqueducts and there is Bollington below you, tucked away in a hollow. Town streets meet at odd angles determined by the geography of the site, so that houses huddle together in tight little clusters. Small industrial concerns have forced their way into the few gaps and topping it all, as you look down from your vantage point on the canal, is the very grand Clarence Mill. People who have never stopped to look at mills often think of them all as much of a muchness, but that they are not. We had passed unadorned Hovis, whimsical Adelphi, where the decoration had been stuck on as an afterthought, and now here we were at Clarence Mill, a building designed quite consciously with an eye to effect. Even with buildings as functional as cotton mills, there is scope for careful design, design that asserts the qualities of height and solidity. The main building is stone-built, five storeys high, just like Adelphi, yet it manages to look much taller. This is because the tall, narrow windows emphasize the height, and the effect is made more powerful by the staircase tower built out over the wharf, an elegant structure that would not be out of place on a chateau. And the same thought must have struck the builders, who have given it a very chateau-ish roof. Then, to complete the vertical theme, there is the tall stack, topped off by little Romanesque arches. The builder who put up this structure in 1854 certainly did his employers proud. The building, incidentally, used to belong to Messrs Brooke and Swindle – not a name to inspire business confidence.

I left the boat on its lofty eminence up on the bank and went down into Bollington, past the tall arch of the aqueduct over Palmerston Street. It was a complex exploration. There are no obvious main roads, but dozens of little streets full of intriguing passages leading to back alleys and hidden courtyards. The main impression is of stony solidity, damp, grey and rain-streaked, but mixed in with this is the exuberance of the Victorian shop fronts, decorated with an almost baroque mass of whirls and curlicues. Each turn of the road provides a fresh view, a new perspective on the town. Even the rain, which seemed to get heavier by the minute, was not enough to dispel the pleasure of a walk round Bollington. It seems odd now, but it is only in recent years that we have been able to find any pleasure at all in these small industrial communities. Perhaps we needed the tower blocks and the industrial estates to bring us back to an appreciation of this more intimate, more human landscape. Now that we have admitted that the tower block was a mistake, socially as well as visually, we have had to return to places like Bollington as starting points from

which we can learn to build again. Good, then, to find that this area, centred on the canal, has been made into a Conservation Area. The Report on the Macclesfield Canal Conservation Area spells out some of the basic rules. Demolition will not be allowed in the area unless re-use is impossible, and all plans for new buildings must contain full details – no more passing of outlines. 'A high standard of designs for new buildings and extensions will be expected, taking due regard of the need to be sympathetic to the materials, form and scale of the area as a whole and the immediate surroundings in particular.' Bravo, but why do we have to create a special area before we begin to insist on good design? Think of the horrors we might have been spared if such rules had been generally applicable.

At the end of the canal the scene closes in briefly at Marple, where new houses spread further and further from the centre. Often in such areas one is given the feeling of being an unwelcome intruder, kept at bay behind high fences, and even barbed wire is not unknown. But Marple seems to have taken to the canal. Gardens run right down to the water. There are boats everywhere, from canal narrow boats to canoes and home-made rafts. Sensibly, however, most of them were moored, leaving the way clear for us, the only boat on the move through the downpour. We reached the junction with the Peak Forest Canal and had a decision to take: whether to admit defeat and stop there for the rest of the day or to work on down through the sixteen Marple locks. The cold wind had dropped, and there comes a point when you are so

At Marple, the canal swoops down through a flight of locks: the warehouse at the side has a boat hole, allowing vessels to pass inside the warehouse to be loaded or unloaded in the dry.

wet you cannot get any wetter, and you might just as well carry on. So carry on we did.

Marple locks have a good deal to commend them. For a start, they are among the most recent to be restored to use, largely as a result of a lot of hard work by the amateur navvies of the Peak Forest Canal Society – to whom many thanks. Without wanting to appear to carp, there is one disadvantage, in that paddle gear had to be taken as and where it could be begged, borrowed – or acquired by other means. The result is a hotchpotch of gear, some very efficient, some over which it would be charitable to remain silent. But having visited these locks several times in the past when they were derelict, perhaps one should forget the criticism and just applaud the fact that we can now travel this way at all.

The locks begin in the town, in a strangely open and quite unprotected setting. One is so used to urban canals being cut off from everything around them that it is quite a shock to find them simply standing by the roadside. The pounds act as ornamental pools for the lucky householders who can sit in their living rooms, looking out through picture windows at the absurdly bobbing ducks, like a permanent cartoon festival. The locks themselves are narrow and startlingly deep, and they drop you over two hundred feet down to the Goyt valley. That makes for something of an exciting passage, and there are visual pleasures too: the neat little stone bridges that cross the tails of the locks; the warehouse with its covered loading bay, and the nearby toll cottage that once governed the carriage of goods to and from the canal; the horse tunnel under the road, with its steep flight of stone stairs down to the lock tail, like steps to a dungeon; the line of the locks, running the waterway out of the town and down towards the open country, crossed by the dry stone walls straggling to the horizon.

If I was to choose one spot that typifies the character of the canal and of Marple, I would pick the section by the warehouse. I would choose the warehouse itself, not only for its combination of well thought out design and attractive appearance, but because this is what the canal is all about. It was here that the local mill owner, Samuel Oldknow, kept his goods and it was Oldknow who was mainly responsible for getting this canal started. He was one of those ambitious men whose drive kept the industrial revolution in top gear, who disregarded obstacles, human as well as physical. Little enough sentiment was involved in the buildings of canals, and if you look across from the warehouse to the little lock cottage, you'll find that there's not much sentimentality in local building styles either. The walls are random rubble, big uneven blocks of stone, crudely hacked to size then packed together; the doorway is no more than a rough rectangle defined by stone slabs; and the small windows have the same, rugged solidity – stone lintels, stone mullions. There is no refinement, but there is a feeling of great strength, a sense of belonging to the land. The stone you can see in the walls is the same stone you see poking through on the surrounding hillsides. Men came to a fundamentally hostile country and simply forced it into answering their own needs. Standing there in the rain, I felt that this one place told me a lot about why I come back to the canals and why I come back to the north. A drenching seemed a small price to pay.

At the bottom of the flight we moored, finally peeled off all those sodden clothes, and celebrated the end of the day with a feast – no common canal fry up, but a real dinner of roast pheasant helped on its way with plentiful supplies of chianti. Amazing how quickly the miserable recollections of cold and rain vanish. We ended the first day of Spring in better spirits than we began it.

CHAPTER 6

Of Shoes and Ships and Sealing Wax – and Aeroplanes and Ice

From our overnight moorings, we had only a few hundred yards to travel before we came out on to the magnificent Marple aqueduct that carries the canal almost a hundred feet above the river Goyt, with its steep, wooded banks. It is not difficult to imagine what a spectacular achievement this must have seemed when it was first built. How they must have stared at the sight of boats passing high over their heads, far above the tallest trees; what a marvel to have one river at your feet, and a second in the air. The aqueduct has three arches, and people sometimes think that the circular holes in the stonework above the arches are there for decoration. Not so. The spandrels were pierced in this way to lighten the load on the pillars without sacrificing the strength of the structure and that was quite the latest thing in engineering techniques when Marple was being built. Yet how soon the wonder of one age can be overshadowed by the greater wonder of the next. The railway viaduct was soon there, looking down on the aqueduct, and the speeding passengers could scoff at the slow, old-fashioned boats. Perhaps Marple Aqueduct is not quite the wonder it once was, but there is still a thrill, the sense that you are defying the laws of nature by taking your boat across this airy waterway.

With the aqueduct behind you, you soon come to the three-hundred-yard Hyde tunnel, which has a curious elliptical arch as an opening and an even curiouser inside. Either the surveyors went wrong or the tunnellers were permanently drunk, but it is certainly a very long way from being straight. The far end of the tunnel could be said to mark the start of the run towards Manchester. It is all very different from the approach to Birmingham, and not just because you are travelling downhill instead of up. Marple is just one of the small towns built around the cotton mills that sprang up in the late eighteenth century, dotting the route into the city, Cottonopolis itself. Rain and Manchester are traditional companions and you could say that it is the notorious rain that made the place. Rain means water for ponds, streams and rivers, and to the early cotton masters that meant power to turn the new machines. So all along the hill streams the mills were set, and even when steam power replaced water power there was no great

problem about adaptation. The old mills formed natural nucleii around which the new were gathered. Much of this area of outer Manchester is made up of old cotton towns and villages swallowed up in the general development, or strung out like beads along the lines of the rivers. Development has followed a different line from that in the Midlands but there is at least one thing in common – rubbish. It was not long before we had the weed-hatch up and were busy hacking away at a variety of tangled materials. Bill had one obstinate piece of rubbish, which he struggled with for so long his fingers became numbed in the cold water, and we kept him going by pouring kettlefuls of boiling water down the weed-hatch. Enough of the heat stayed in the area of the hatch to make the icy water just about bearable.

Romiley, Bradley, Woodley, Hyde, the little towns slip past, and so too do the mills. In these parts they appear as bright red cubes: dark and satanic they might have been on the inside, but outside they are positively garish. Many of them have names or simple geometric patterns picked out in yellow brick. Garish, but rather melancholy, like a fairground on a wet day. For the prosperous days have ended for the big cotton mills. Artificial fibres, the growing industry of Asia, have eaten away the guts of Manchester cotton, leaving only these empty frames.

This area is changing fast. Even the geography is changing. At Hyde new road works presented us with the startling illusion of a dead end of sheet piling, which turned out not to be quite that drastic

Fairfield Junction on the Ashton Canal, with its low bridge and there is a clear indication that the canal is penetrating to the heart of the old Lancashire cotton industry.

for a narrow channel had been left between the high metal walls. Beyond that the valley is gradually being filled in, as the Corporation dumps the city's rubbish, to the infinite delight of the seagulls that squawk and wheel round each new cartload. The astonishing thing is that the canal itself is crystal clear, a dubious blessing as you get all too distinct a view of the muck you would otherwise float over in untroubled ignorance.

We reached Dukinfield Junction where the Peak Forest is joined by the Huddersfield Narrow Canal, and the closed-in world of the city and heavy industry really begin to dominate the scene. Yet even here you can look out behind you to see the open hills, freshly dusted with snow. This may be a good area to get away from, but at least there is somewhere to go. The last lap into Manchester itself is down the eighteen locks of the Ashton Canal. This canal has been improved out of all recognition by the combined efforts of the waterways authority and local industries, such as Anchor Chemicals. The idea has been to improve the scene for the benefit of everyone – for those, like ourselves, who just pass through and for the local people who can stroll along the towpath or take a lunchtime break by the water. Yet somehow things have gone sadly wrong. It looks right – newly painted balance beams, bollards, heel-grips to make the job of pushing the beam easier, good chunky stone surrounds at locks. It looks fine, but just wait until you start using it. You put your back to a balance beam and start trudging backwards – and then trip over and land flat on the ground because the bollard has been placed right in the middle of the walkway. You want to cross the lock to open the far gate and you find there's no handrail, so you either have to go the long way round or do a precarious balancing act along the top of the gates. Then there is the new hydraulic gear: a marvel on the drawing board, a disastrous time-wasting menace in practice, and, as we were to discover later, a dangerous one. My guess is that whoever put this lot together was not used to working a boat through a lock. A good scheme to look at. Such a shame it doesn't match its looks in performance.

If you find time to look around while working the locks, you get a good idea of just how much Manchester owes to its industrial revolution past – or perhaps it would be fairer to say, how much Britain's industrial revolution owed to Manchester. It was here among the tall chimneys and mean terraces that the price was paid for the new prosperity. Yet the houses retained their human scale, bred real communities and have a few qualities that have too often been ignored in recent times. But we must beware of becoming too sentimental about

the past, of becoming like a flock of Orwellian sheep, endlessly bleating 'all old good, all new bad'. For what we are seeing are the survivors, the houses that were built solidly enough to remain standing over the years. What we no longer see, thank God, are the crumbling tenements, the appalling cellar houses and the infamous courtyards down by the Irk and Irwell. Some change is all good.

At the bottom of the locks we came to the Rochdale Canal, so I set off in search of a Company official and my licence. The offices stand by a vast wharf in Ducie Street. Once this was a busy, thriving place where the trade of Manchester was carried on. Now it is a car park. The offices themselves have that solid, dignified look that befits a solid, dignified trading concern. They were suspiciously silent. I pressed the 'Enquiries' bell – no answer. I began knocking at a few doors – no answer. I knocked at every door in the place, and then pushed a few open to look inside. No one in sight. It seemed that I had discovered the *Marie Celeste* of the inland waterways. I was not, however, going to wait about. I had paid my £6.50 and I intended to get my money's worth. I cannot honestly claim I got good value for my money, but I can say that I've never known a canal journey like it.

Down the first lock we went, and then immediately disappeared under a tall tower block on Piccadilly, Manchester's main shopping centre. Here we were, right in the heart of the city, and we couldn't see a thing. We could scarcely see each other. And down in this black

In its passage through the centre of Manchester, the Rochdale Canal goes right under a tower block.

hole there was a lock to be worked. The Company claim that the canal has been closed for maintenance, but Heaven knows what they have been doing. Gates creak open in the claustrophobic dark, as you worm your way round the pillars that form the foundation of the great block up above. Then you emerge into the light to find the canal hemmed in by high stone walls. Over the top I could see what appeared to be grimy warehouses, and occasionally caught a glimpse of one of those marvellously ornate, Edwardian commercial buildings, blindingly vulgar in its ostentation, shouting at the world, 'Look how rich I am, and look how rich I intend to stay!' At one point I jumped up on the cabin roof to have a look at what I guessed to be one of the old industrial back streets, only to find, to my astonishment, that I was peering straight into the Playboy Club. I don't know who was more surprised, myself or the white-scutted young lady who suddenly saw a figure appear like a jack-in-the-box from out of the canal.

The rest of Britain might have been suffering from drought, but we had a damn sight more water than we wanted. I have never seen so much water going down a canal. When they built the Rochdale Canal through the city centre, there was no room for niceties like overspill weirs to take away excess water. The result was a torrent that flowed straight over the top of the lock gates to cascade out over the bottom. What with that and the high walls, it was like travelling down a miniature Grand Canyon. I reckon a competent canoeist could have gone straight down without opening a lock. We had to fight to get the top gates open at all against the flow of water and when Bill went wandering on down the towpath to the next lock, he suddenly found himself being overtaken by a sort of tidal wave as the lock above emptied. He tried to outrun the flow, but it caught him and he soon had water lapping round his ankles. He was not amused. At one lock the flooding had got so bad with all the water that we'd pushed in front of us, that you couldn't see the lock sides at all. It was like driving the boat into the middle of a huge pond, and I jumped off hoping that I was jumping into six inches of water and not six feet. So we thundered down on the flood and the front of the wave carried the rubbish of the city before us like lumber on a Canadian river. Manchester came and Manchester went and we never saw it. We were out the other side before we knew what had hit us.

Our original plan had been to moor somewhere near the city centre, but there was no way we could have stopped back there in the canyon, so we chugged on through the industrial no-man's-land that marks the beginning of the Bridgewater Canal, looking for a suitable spot.

No shortage of water on the Rochdale Canal in the heart of Manchester.

We rounded a corner and there, on the side of the canal, stood an aeroplane – not some light aircraft that had been blown off course, but a genuine, full-sized Comet airliner. We had just about got over that shock, when we saw that beyond it was a ship, an actual ocean-going ship. The quayside was piled high with objects that looked remarkably like beer barrels. It seemed we had found our moorings.

At least the presence of the ship told us where we were, down by the Pomona Docks on the Manchester Ship Canal, and a little investigation solved the mystery of aeroplane and ship. The latter was a worthy vessel with a long and respectable history which included a spell as the Isle of Wight ferry and a day of glory at Dunkirk. It has been saved from the wreckers to do duty as a pub-cum-nightclub-cum-discotheque, and very popular it seemed to be too. The Comet was due to find a new life as a restaurant, a plan which seemed to me quite lunatic. Think of aeroplanes and you think of cramped seats and plastic food on plastic trays. Who in their right minds would actually choose to go out for an evening to eat in an aeroplane?

We saw little enough of Manchester in our startling descent, but the need to catch up on our shopping gave us an opportunity to see what we had missed. I have always had an affection for the place but, like the majority of British cities, Manchester has undergone some violent changes in the last quarter-century. When I first knew it, it was still essentially Cottonopolis, the thriving commercial centre of the textile industry. The warehouses, the brokers' offices, the Exchange – they set the pattern. The city was a reflection of the untroubled optimism of the Victorian entrepreneurs, and even the names, such as Free Trade Hall, set you to thinking of the old days of undeniable vigour. Inevitably it has now got its share of second-rate developments, wan imitations of the international style, but they've not destroyed that energy yet. Manchester can still boast the finest neo-Gothic building in the country, the Town Hall, blessed by a fine open setting. And around that are a cluster of streets that offer a mixture of old and new, and in this part of the city at least the mixture works. Look at the Bank of America, which is a building of real quality, uncompromisingly modern in concept, yet never jarring with the pattern of buildings around it. This is real 'development', deserving of the name which, sadly, has become one of the most debased words in our vocabulary.

Back to the canal, and you get the other perspective of the city, the seedy run-down area where the wealth that is celebrated in the city centre was generated. Having struggled to cope with 'modern' canals, here we are back at the very beginning of the canal age, on a wide, deep,

An old Comet makes a unique restaurant beside the canal in Manchester.

trouble-free waterway. This was the first British canal to take a line that owed nothing to any natural water course and it is still impressive, even though its most famous original feature has gone. At the opening in 1761, the aqueduct that carried the canal over the River Irwell was claimed as the marvel of the age, the eighth wonder of the world. It has gone, and so too has the Irwell, for the old river has been swallowed up by the Ship Canal. In place of the old aqueduct, however, is a new wonder, and we arrived at Barton just in time to see it in use.

A coaster was coming down the Ship Canal, and the aqueduct which carries the Bridgewater was closed off by gates at either end. Slowly, but so smoothly that the surface of the water scarcely quivered, the whole aqueduct began to move, pivoting on a single central pillar. Sixteen hundred tons, that's what the trough weighs when it is full of water, and it slid along, the weight shared between rollers and a hydraulic ram, and scarcely a drop was spilt as the structure swung away to clear the main channel then back to allow us to cross. It is a great tribute to Leader Williams and his workers of the 1880s. You can still see the abutments of the original aqueduct; and I did wonder what those ladies and gentlemen who came to marvel in 1761 would have said if they could have seen it today.

The canal now took us up to the spot that can reasonably claim to be the birthplace of all our canals, Worsley. It was here that the Duke of Bridgewater had his mines, and it was thanks to the stubborn stupidity of the owners of the Irwell Navigation who refused to offer

Crossing the Manchester Ship Canal on the Barton swing aqueduct.

him reasonable terms for the transport of his coal, that he decided to build his canal from Worsley to Manchester. The success of the Duke, his agent Gilbert and the engineer Brindley in overcoming the practical difficulties of canal building encouraged others to follow. There was still more encouragement when the canal was opened and the Duke was able to cut the price of his coal exactly in half.

You get very little hint of mining or any other industry in Worsley today, which has more the air of a quaint, old-world backwater, with its greenery and old black and white buildings. The only clue comes from the colour of the water, tinged bright orange from the ore in the workings. But if you follow a little side arm, you come to Worlsey Delph itself, a hole in the hillside, insignificant, disappointing really, giving no hint that behind the entrance he miles of underground passages where the boats used to drift right up to the coal face itself.

We came upon a strange phenomenon at Worsley, which I can only describe as undredging. It is common enough to see muck being taken out of the canal, but never before have I seen anyone putting it back in – not officially, anyway. It is all due to those mines: to counteract the subsidence, the bottom of the canal has periodically to be raised up again. Wide, flat boats are towed up piled high with dirt, then a hose, powerful enough to send a jet of water sixty feet into the air, is used to wash the whole lot overboard. We followed one of the empty boats out under the motorway to the flat, eerie landscape of Chat Moss.

Chat Moss, a great bog, an undrained wasteland, was a great challenge to the canal engineers. They managed to get their canal across, but not much else has happened in the area. Normally I enjoy a feeling of space around me, but there's nothing inviting about Chat Moss. It is an empty land, dead, sterile. Views stretch over to wide horizons, and in the distance you see that strange, Meccano construction, a colliery headstock. Astley Green Colliery is now as dead as the land on which it stands. The headstock is idle, the enginehouse in ruins. Only the village remains. Mournful terraces line the main street that points meaninglessly to the flashes and the spoil, to the dead mine. Once those last remains of the pit are cleared, how strange that village will seem, removed from the only thing that gave it life.

Leigh is the first town of any size that you meet, and you need no specialized knowledge to recognize it as a cotton town. Tall chimneys punctuate the route with the regularity of poplars on a French country road. The chimneys stand, but the smoke no longer drifts from their tops. The mills are derelict, or at best, half used. Windows are broken, decay has set in. Two hundred years ago the mills of Lancashire

The canalside colliery at Plank Lane that once provided the canal with a busy trade.

Michael Ware had joined the original trio for this part of the journey.

took over cotton manufacture for the world, and the old suppliers of India and the Far East suffered. Now the East thrives and Lancashire declines. A sort of rough justice prevails.

Beyond Leigh the busily wheeling headstock gear of Bickershaw colliery tells you that this pit at least is far from finished. A big modern colliery this, but above ground there is little sign of change. A gantry still looks like a gantry, whether on a busy mine or a dead one. They still use steam locomotives at the pit, and why not? The one thing you're never short of at the pit-head is coal for the boilers, so it makes economic sense. You have to take a bit more trouble than you would with a diesel; you need time to get an engine into steam. Once you are under way, though, you have a cheap and dependable machine to command. Until quite recently, another old transport system was in use here as well. Coal from the pit was loaded up at the colliery staithes and sent by the canal down to the power station at Wigan.

With modernization that all came to an end, and another fleet of lorries joined the overcrowded roads.

We had no intention of stopping at Bickershaw, but the swing-bridge that carries the main road was locked for the night so there was no choice. I suppose few people would choose to moor up outside a working colliery but it has its compensations. At night, you see the other face of the pit. It takes on a whole new character. The dirt of the colliery yard is lost in the shadows. Details disappear, only the big, strong shapes stand out, looming mysterious through the billowing steam.

Once past Bickershaw we were back with that flat desolation, where the only rises in the land are made by the piles of industrial spoil. The morning wind keened over this wilderness and, with the canal slightly raised above the surrounding ground, there was no shelter from it. Spring it may have been, but there was a quarter of an inch of ice on the canal. Ducks skidded and slithered while we forced a way through. Where the ice was thinnest we passed with a hiss and a crackle, but where it lay thick there was a deep grating sound, a rumble along the hull. It broke off at the bows in thick chunks, but as the waves spread out to the bank the ice gave like thick plastic sheeting, buckled, then settled back into place. The cold wind, the empty land, offered no cheer, and the sight of Wigan power station at least offered a promise of change, a new town to see, a new route to take as we turned east on to the Leeds and Liverpool Canal.

CHAPTER 7

The Cotton Kingdom

You can't go to Wigan without visiting Wigan pier. I once heard a Mayor of Wigan, who should have known better, insist that the pier doesn't exist. But it's there all right. Admittedly, there is not a great deal left to see, just a hump at the bottom of the locks that marks the site where passengers once embarked for the boat to Liverpool – a halfpenny for every two miles, it used to cost them. They used to get on the boat at seven in the morning and reach Liverpool at three in the afternoon; or they could get off at Scaris - brook if they felt like a spot of sea air and take the coach down to Southport. But that was a long time ago. The railways put an end to the old passenger service, and now the pier has gone. But the old warehouses that surround the basin are still there, only recently saved from demolition. It is a place full of character, yelling out for new uses that will keep its character intact.

We returned to the boat to find a window gone, a pile of glass on the cabin floor and £10 missing. No one was in sight except for a steeplejack at the very top of the tall stack of the power station on the opposite bank. One thing was certain: he didn't run down the ladders, nick ten quid and dash back up again in twenty minutes. So we set off to find a glazier and take a look round Wigan, one of the cheerier episodes in an increasingly gloomy day.

Wigan, like its pier, sounds a bit of a joke to those who don't know it. Yet it turns out to be a pleasant sort of a place, full of good, robust building, but with enough touches of eccentricity to keep it thoroughly interesting. The Victorian shop fronts tend towards extravagant decoration, and the upper storeys can boast a whole world of architectural embellishment, from black and white Tudor to elaborate, almost baroque, red brick. Wigan may owe much of its prosperity to coal and the industrial revolution, but this is no urban parvenu. It got its first charter from Henry III, back in 1246, so while it is no surprise to find a town that has grown up around the old centres of church and market cross, it is a pleasure to find the old centres recognized, appreciated and lately cleaned. The church has something of the whole town in it. The main structure is of rough-hewn stone, a bit coarse at first glance, but if you look more closely you find a wealth of finely wrought detail. I do not know if the builders of the church went in for conscious symbolism, but the base, near the ground, is roughest, closest to its origins, while as the building climbs towards the sky, it seems to become more delicate, take on a more spiritual air, until it reaches the final exultation of the spire.

Wigan has two markets, one new, one old. The new one is called a market, but it's not a proper one at all, just a group of large stores clustered together to keep out of the way of the weather. It is very clean, very convenient and the local shopkeepers spruce it up with flowers at the ends of the escalators. The trouble is, such places tend to be entirely occupied by the supermarkets and the big multiples, so that there is an overall blandness about them. You could never say that about the old market. The stalls themselves have a rich variety to offer. There are books and clothes, pots and pans. The stall holders shout their wares, protesting that at the prices they are charging all they can look forward to is a pauper's grave. But the emphasis is very much on food, and the locals certainly seem to like their victuals. Here among the butchers, the fishmongers, the greengrocers and bakers are the pie shops and chippies, and a stall that loudly announces its special, and indeed only, wares – tripe, cowheel and pigs' trotters. And if the crowds are anything to judge by, the people of Wigan love it.

We braced ourselves for the daunting prospect of the long climb up the twenty-one locks of the Wigan flight with a glass of ale in a pub that was rich with Victorian mahogany and shining brass. It was as well we took that bracer, for we certainly needed it. As we started up the locks, the rain started down: not even down, really, more horizontal, blown flat by a cold wind. Working a flight of locks in the rain is not much fun, and when the locks are right pigs that don't want to be worked in the first place it is least fun of all. And that's what we got at Wigan. Half the paddle gear was out of order. The jack cloughs, big wooden levers that slide covers across the faces of the sluices, seldom worked. Many of the rest had to be heaved and bullied and cajoled into working. And just to make it that much more difficult, all the gear was locked and chained to preserve it from vandalism. We were constantly fumbling with keys and locks, fastening and unfastening the chains with numb fingers. It was sheer misery. We must have looked like a collection of little clouds coming up the hill. The cold rain combined with hot sweaty bodies to give each of us his own, personal aureole of steam. Three and a half hours that flight took us, and what did we see on the way? Precious little, apart from a factory that described itself as a waste manufacturer. I'd always suspected they existed. As we reached the top, the lock keeper came out and asked us if we meant to go on. No, we said, that was not our intention. Right, he said, you can tie up right where you are, so we simply fastened the boat up to the top gate and called it a day. Down in the cabin, I peeled off the sodden clothes and listened to the news on the radio. Britain, it said, was suffering from a severe drought. I switched off. Is there any pleasure in that sort of travel? Well, like the man banging his head against a brick wall, it's great when you stop.

The splendours of the scenery above Wigan more than compensated for the rain that was still with us the next day. One of the great attractions of this part of the world is the speed with which you can make the transition from town to country. That climb of more than two hundred feet up Wigan locks had marked the end of the flat land. To describe the country we were coming to as a rolling landscape would be to give quite the wrong impression. This is hill country, yes, but it tends to come in spasms. A gentle hill is suddenly split by a steep rift as a fast stream slices into the land; that smooth slope is topped by a ragged outline of broken crags. It is a discontinuous landscape, but for all that it can have its harmonies. The grey houses and the dry stone walls seem rooted in the land, and even the many remains of the early mills seem natural and at home here. We came through a wooded cutting, down the sides of which the streams splashed busily, then the land opened out below us and there down in the hollow was the typically tall, narrow shape of an eighteenth-century mill. The streams still collect in the old mill pond, terraced into the hillside. Once that water fell on to the water wheel, powering the busy spinning frames. There is a later addition too, a tall stack that marks the coming of steam and the end of the isolated factories in the hills. They are mostly abandoned now, the old mills, lonely reminders that these first buildings of the industrial revolution were at one with their surroundings.

This is rough country. The deformed, bent trees are indication enough of where the weather comes from in this part of the world. Yet in its severity, its uncompromising nature, it has a true beauty. Such a landscape deserves buildings as robust as itself, and blessedly it often gets them. The early mills, the isolated farms, even the railway viaduct in rustic stone, all seem entirely appropriate. Small towns such as Adlington are equally fitting. Their builders knew from experience that such a country and such a climate demand to be taken seriously, so they fitted the pattern of the building to the shape of the land and made close groups that kept the wind and rain at bay. And because the design is so closely determined by natural forces, the towns themselves seem like organic things, grown up out of the land rather than simply set down upon it.

The rain finally gave up in time for the little flight of locks at Johnson's Hillocks, every bit as delightful as the name suggests. You pass under a motorway bridge but, although the hum of traffic can still be heard, it does nothing to detract from the purely rural atmosphere. The walls and shrubs that usually screen a canal end and the scene opens out before you. Here are the hillocks which give the spot its name, crowned by a copse of tall trees. Through these humps the canal weaves a gently curving path, and the artificial canal structures seem in some way to fit perfectly into this very natural world. The overspill weirs send water coursing and bubbling in fair imitation of a hill stream, while the bridges are no more than single baulks of timber laid across the water. I found the scene endearing, but Bill was less enthusiastic when he slipped from one of my charming bridges into the stream. My own joy was complete with the discovery that everything at the locks worked. If I hadn't already felt that I was now really coming home, then the lunchtime stop at Riley Green would have convinced me – hot pot and mushy peas. When I see mushy peas I know I'm back. Heaven knows what the attraction is in that startling green mess. Perhaps it is just a stirring of old memories. Tripe or Yorkshire pud have much the same effect, but there is something very homely about mushy peas that puts them in a class of their own.

Wigan Pier was not an invention of George Orwell's: it exists and here it is.

From Johnson's Hillocks to Blackburn, a town that starts in a hollow, but steadily climbs out up the surrounding hills. We took a high route along one rim of the bowl, and the impression was of endless terraces, striding in even ranks up the slopes. Seen close at hand, they are a mixture of sad dereliction and desperate cheerfulness. Many houses are decked out in gaudy colours, but too often the rows lead to nothing but a dreary waste. Down in the valley, the chimneys soar. I remember driving out of Blackburn very early one morning, when the whole hollow was filled with mist and only those chimneys poked through, pinnacles in a grey sea. Now even the chimneys are beginning to decay, and many are already leaning at most unlikely angles. Once they stood by factories that were the pride of Lancashire, with grandiose names like 'Imperial' picked out in the brickwork. At least they keep a sense of humour in these parts. Halfway up one of the tall chimneys, someone has painted the slogan 'Harry was h –', and the phrase ends in an ominous vertical trickle of paint down the stack.

You need a sense of humour in Blackburn to cope with what's happening to the place. In the centre, the tower blocks rule. The tall chimneys can seem almost natural, tapering upwards from a broad base that itself springs from the massive bulk of the mill, but the flats just look like oversize building blocks dropped around aimlessly by a careless giant. Only the church spires can begin to compete for a place on the Blackburn skyline.

Blackburn epitomizes a certain type of unthinking development. Wigan was a place with a long history, developed over the centuries. It was cotton that called Blackburn into being. The demands of the mill were all important. Homes were no more than places for mill workers to sleep and eat. Terraces kept nice and handy for the mill, that's what Blackburn wanted. This was the ugliest face of the industrial revolution: people reduced to work units. The tower blocks follow in the same tradition. The planners think in terms of units – dwelling units, family units. And still no one asked the people if that was what they wanted.

Blackburn locks showed us oldest Blackburn, built when stone was still the cheapest building material, before canal and rail brought in the bricks. Now the mills are dead, the canal given over to pleasure boats. On we went through the dripping land, on a winding route that stuck to the natural contours, past the power station, incongruous in its moorland setting, and on past the inevitable accompaniment of the northern industrial town, the allotments. In this part of the world, allotments also mean pigeon lofts. They are small miracles of ingenuity.

Anything can take its place in the building of a pigeon loft, any material can be fitted in and any unwanted object made to serve. Keep your eyes open and it's amazing what you'll find pressed into service. Wasn't that a pensioned-off tram car? It was indeed.

The day ended at Clayton-le-Moors, a place whose name carries a promise of pastoral delights that quite fail to materialize. Instead you get down-at-heel industry and a first impression of overall dullness. But if you stay on you find a genuine community. All that talk about Northern warmth and friendliness has become something of a cliche, but the cliche became a reality that night in the local. The bar had one of those football games where you twiddle knobs to make suspended players kick at the ball. Nowadays, they are made of plastic, but this was good solid wood, and that old 5-3-2-1 line-up told you it was well past the first bloom of youth. We played, inexpertly, then sat back to watch two locals give an expert demonstration. Their skill and shapely paunches suggested they were no strangers to the pub. We finished up joining in their game and chatting as informally and openly as I would in my own village pub back home. The two men were locals, born and bred in the town. They used to live next door to each other in a very slummy neighbourhood, where the houses were so bad the two lads used to talk together through a crack in the partition wall.

Nowhere on the journey did the textile mills crowd round the canal in quite the way they do in Burnley.

The conditions were dreadful, but neither of them ever wanted to move away from the area. They feel there is a quality about the life they have which they don't want to lose. Back to the cliches, then – back to homeliness and friendliness. Yet they were surely right, just as those who cleared away the squalor of the slums were right to do so. What is sad is that, in so many cases, when they cleared away the slums, they cleared away the community with them. It is easier to build bathrooms than neighbourliness.

Morning fragility was eased by the sight of fair weather. Cumulus piled high over the hills. From there the clouds drifted on, a stately white armada. Our route was high up among those hills, and to keep a level the canal was forced to twist and turn, almost doubling back on itself to round the high ground. Down below we could see the mills dotted along the river as we made our tortuous progress towards Burnley. You slide into the town through the six-hundred-yard Gannow tunnel, and you emerge into a world hemmed in by the crumbling mills of the late eighteenth and early nineteenth centuries. You get no sense of dull uniformity moving among the Lancashire cotton towns. Burnley is about as unlike Blackburn as a town could be. Where the latter is all red brick and tall chimneys, Burnley is predominantly stone. Blackburn offers wide views with the mills scattered across the valley floor; here the industrial scene is constantly closing in on you, shutting off all other views. It is all cotton, cotton, cotton – apart from a brief pause where a tripe processor has slipped in – until you come out by the B.W.B. maintenance yard. After that you set off on the exaggeratedly named Burnley Mile. This is not quite like the Blackpool Mile, it is just a high bank that flanks the town. L. T. C. Rolt once described it as offering the finest industrial view in the country. It did once, perhaps, but not any more. The centre of the town has been ripped out to make way for a new road system and a shopping precinct. They have simply removed the heart of the town and dropped in a sort of standard unit, totally featureless, quite divorced from its surroundings, nothing to do with the geography, history or traditions of Burnley. It was quite a relief to get off the bank and leave it all behind. I liked Burnley's past too much to want to spend long contemplating its present.

At the far end of the bank you come to the park. Parks come in two varieties. There are those that owe a lot to the tradition of the landscape garden, giving that country-come-to-town feeling that you have, for example, in London's Hyde Park. Then there's the Municipal Park, which instead of being country writ small is suburban garden writ large: neat pathways and flower beds; a lake with a well defined shape, usually rather like a ham bone; there might be a clock with the date or some welcoming message picked out in flowers, all beautifully clear and legible. And, best of all, there might be a band stand, very ornate and ready for the Sunday concert. Burnley's park is definitely Municipal, a bit prim, rather pompous and very slightly absurd. Like so many of our native institutions, though, the Municipal Park holds on to its place in the memory. I can recall so vividly those outings to feed the ducks. I can remember the fete day with the donkey rides, when I slipped from the saddle into a pile of manure and was led home howling and aromatic. And the bands, prize silver and brass; men with red faces bulging over tight, bright uniform collars; *William Tell* and *Poet and Peasant*. There's a lot to be said for the Municipal Park.

The canal writhes on, past the town of Nelson, a name which for me will always be associated with its greatest honorary citizen, Sir Learie Constantine. When English counties were limited to homegrown cricketers, the Lancashire League took in the best, and none was better than Constantine, for so long the favourite son of this sprawling, industrial town. Beyond Nelson, the canal rises through the attractive Barrowford flight of locks, a popular spot with sightseers on sunny weekends, before disappearing into Foulridge tunnel. It is just short of a mile long, and they do say – there are photographs to prove it – that a cow which fell in the canal once swam right through the tunnel, and had to be revived with brandy when it got to the far end. Rather the cow than me, but I do admire its good sense in stopping at Foulridge. It is a marvellous place, a little Pennine village, crouched down in the lee of a hill, the stone cottages in the centre huddled tight round the tiny village green. It exists, quite a secret little place, between the road and the canal, and it seems all the better for being tucked away and private. You sense right away that that tunnel has marked some kind of divide. The industrial cotton towns are behind you, the open farming land and the moors lie ahead. You are into the heart of the Pennines.

CHAPTER 8

Pennine Way

The day we set out to cross the Pennines was the day, above all others, I would have wished to see the sun shine, not so much for myself, for I had been this way before, but for the others to whom it was all new. As a native I feel a certain proprietorial pride for what I consider to be as fine a stretch of country as you'll ever see from a canal. There the route winds, in a series of complex contortions, to fit an equally complex range of small hillocks, with the taller Pennine hills beyond. As we set off, it seemed that my wish was being ignored.

At first, however, the route continued to follow the western flank of the valley. Over to the east you can see Kelbrook, built on the lower slopes of Kelbrook Moor, and suffering from an acute case of schizophrenia. On the one side, there is the old village, grey stone houses clustered on the hillside, close as a clenched fist. Next to it is a new development. White weather-boarding gleams out, and houses are laid in neat rows, spaced out to meet an ideal of suburban propriety. Coming into Bamoldswick is even more dispiriting. Here the canal is lined with that peculiar brand of council house, built shortly after the last war, and notable for its unique drabness. The houses of dull concrete looked unlovely and unloved and they were separated from us by a high wire fence, intended either to keep us out or the locals in. The gardens were, without exception, as unkempt and forlorn as the houses, as though the appalling dreariness of the place had drained all the spirit from the people. Then, just by the bridge, the old estate gave way to a new development of little square houses, stone faced and most attractive. That stone will improve with the years, while the concrete will just go on getting duller. So we came out of Bamoldswick on an optimistic note, and headed towards my favourite flight of locks. And, right on cue, the sun came out.

Greenberfield locks are, quite simply, beautiful. The canal twists and falls in a wide curve round a high, grassy hill. Every single element here fits, nothing jars. The little lock cottage is a perfect example of Pennine vernacular: random rubble walls, stone lintels and mullions. No decorative effects and none needed, for the stone itself carries in it a world of rich texture and colour. Light breaks and splinters on the rough surface or glints straight back at you from the smooth slabs that surround all the openings. The one, solitary addition is a little sundial on the wall, which still carries the date, 1824. Everything else at Greenberfield shows the same common-sense approach. The stone bridges are definitely neat, not gaudy and the wooden footbridges are masterpieces of practical simplicity. Even the lock keeper who came out for a chat fitted in, as plain and commonsensical as his surroundings. He was friendly, cheerful and quite plainly loved his work. He was in a place he liked, meeting enough people to provide company but never enough to make a crowd. He was independent, taking pride in doing a good job well. I expect this can seem a lonely, desolate place in a harsh winter, but on a sunny spring day he seemed a man to envy.

Here in the hills you meet two recurring and connected themes – dry stone walls and sheep. The low walls straggle across the slopes, marking off the winter grazing from the open moor. The sheep spread everywhere, long-haired, grey creatures, like slowly trundling boulders, with their awkward lambs tottering around them. The lambs seem very tentative about life at this age, but a sudden moment of boldness can overcome them and they leap high in the air, then stand stock still, rather overwhelmed by their own audacity. This is very much Pennine country, and to emphasize the point, the Pennine Way itself briefly takes over the towpath near East Marton. What curious anomalies the

The Leeds & Liverpool Canal climbs across the Pennines through a series of wide locks.

changing times produce. The walker, who has really nothing at all to do with the canal, takes over the towpath, while horses, the creatures it was built for in the first place, are actually banned from using it. Here the canal goes into its most violent convulsions, writing a great letter 'W' on the land. We had the water to ourselves, but it is very odd on a busy day to look out across the valley and see a boat you are following apparently pointing straight towards you.

Bank Newton locks take you down from the heights and here we met the first moving boats we had seen for some time. Half-way down the flight a hire base has been made out of an old warehouse, and very well made too, though I must confess to a twinge of resentment at having to wait around for other boats. We had had it too good for too long. From here it is a straggle of locks down to Gargrave, the most northerly point of our journey, and straggles like that always seem hard work. The sun had gone again, the grey cold was back, and suddenly the day seemed very long and very tiring. We were really delighted to reach Skipton. And when we got into the centre of the town, we saw something that turned delight into pure, unsullied joy – a pump-out. Only those who have ever had to travel with a loo they can't use and, worse still, can't empty, can begin to appreciate the rapture of that moment. The day was crowned with glory.

I think if I had to select just one town to illustrate the qualities that I admire most, then I should choose Skipton. What sort of town is it? Market town or industrial town? Is it built around the lands of some great aristocratic family, or does it draw its wealth from the sheep on the surrounding hills and the trade in wool? The answer is that it is all these things at once, and more. Nikolaus Pevsner in his *Buildings of England* notes: 'There is little here that needs singling out', and, in a way, he is right, for what marks Skipton is its marvellous coherence, its overall unity of material and style that enables the mill to sit at ease by the castle. We came in through that part of the town that the tourist visiting 'The Gateway to the Dales' seldom, if ever, sees. Here the square blocks of the spinning mills stand beside the long, low weaving sheds. These sheds all have a saw-tooth roof line, for the light in the sheds comes from overhead, north-facing roof lights. But this outline is usually hidden away behind the end wall, which is blank apart from a multiplicity of drainpipes descending from a multiplicity of gutters. Blank but not dull. A big, stone wall is never dull, a fact we easily recognize if we change the context and go to another part of Skipton where we can look up at another featureless stone wall on the castle. Here it is common enough to wax enthusiastic and speak of the wall as

towering or dramatic or monumental. I suggest that it is the intrinsic quality of the stone that gives the pleasure, and we can find that as well in the mill as in the castle.

How smoothly you make the transition between the different elements of Skipton. We came out from among the mills to arrive at the wharf with its old warehouses now converted to cater to the pleasure-boat trade. And after that pump-out we moored right in the centre of the town, without noticing the least change in style in the buildings. We walked on down the Springs Branch that leads past a splendid conversion of industrial buildings into houses, and out under those walls of Skipton Castle. Well, there is no denying that it is dramatic, and nowhere does it seem more so than here, where it drops sheer down to the water. It is certainly more dramatic than when seen from the main entrance, where two portly round towers stand as chubby guardians to the gate. Seen from the canal, the castle really does look like a fourteenth-century fortification; seen from the main entrance it is the seventeenth-century modernization that predominates. It is a fine building, and inside it is as thoroughly romantic as any self respecting castle should be.

The Springs Branch could easily be mistaken for a moat, or even a quiet stream in a wooded glade, but the peace and beauty are modern arrivals. Once the water was busy with boats and the air was hazy with dust, as stone was loaded from the tramway that led off to the nearby

These neat footbridges across locks are a feature of the Leeds & Liverpool.

quarry. Industry, of a sort, has even older roots here. In between the canal and the river is an old grain mill and its mill pond. There has been a mill here since the twelfth century. Eight hundred years of use and there is still a miller at work in Skipton.

The main street, just the sort of fine, wide street you would expect to find in a market town, leads away from the church. And, like all market towns, it is very liberally supplied with pubs. The buildings that line this street are mostly Georgian and Victorian, and the shop fronts have a strong Victorian character, complete with faded gold lettering announcing wares at prices that are, alas, no longer quite accurate. Houses, industry, castle and church meet and mingle with no sense of incongruity. Antique shop and fish-and-chip shop seem equally at home. It is a town of few pretensions, a working town, a town of remarkable unity, set on the edge of some of the finest scenery in Britain. That is a combination that is hard to beat.

When you look at the map, you might think you would have an easy time of it after Skipton. Twelve miles to go before you meet another lock. You would be in for a sad disappointment. Locks there are not: swing bridges there are. Lots and lots of swing bridges. Some need little effort to shift them, but others … well, it keeps you fit. For the rest of its length, the Leeds and Liverpool Canal follows the line of the Aire Valley, at first high up on the northern slope, where the view changes from wide vistas to narrow passages through small towns and villages. Kildwick is the most obviously attractive, offering a rich assortment of buildings. At one end of the spectrum is Kildwick Hall, stately but rather dour, while at the other there is a row of houses that back on to the canal, their walls dropping sheer to the water. Like most of the small places in these parts, Kildwick is homogeneous, compact, all of a piece.

By the time you get to Silsden, industry is creeping up with a vengeance. Lancashire cotton has now given way to Yorkshire wool, and in a county which boasts all kinds and varieties of sheep from the commonplace to the exotic, it is not hard to see why. Then industry, too, fades in favour of a sort of smeared-out suburbia, and just at the moment when you risk becoming bored by the monotony of it, the long pound ends with one of the great dramatic moments of canal travel. At Bingley the canal suddenly charges off down the hill by means of what was once called the Great Lock and is now, more prosaically, called the Bingley Five. Stand at the top, and the canal below looks as though it must be a different waterway, the drop is so great. The locks here form a staircase; in other words you go down the top lock, and when the

bottom gates open, they give, not on to another pound, but straight on to the next lock. In a hundred yards or so, you drop down sixty feet. There are other staircases in the system, but none that combines such broad locks with such a plummeting descent, none where you open a paddle to produce such a thundering cascade. Mind you, we were doing it the easy way, going downhill. You simply use your one lockful of water to fill the next lock and so you go on, riding the same water on down the five locks. Coming up is a different matter, more complicated. The old retired lengthman who fives in the top cottage at Bingley admits that even he can't understand the written instructions. The basic thing to remember is that you have to keep topping up the lock above you to get up.

Most of what I know about Bingley has come from talking to this old lengthman, who has been there since the First World War. He first pointed out to me the strange portions of faded lettering on his house, a bit of an 'L' here, a bit of a 'P' there. The explanation for the letters is that when the house was being built, the Company had just knocked down one of their warehouses at Liverpool, which had, of course, got the name of the Company painted on the front. No one bothered about that when it came to re-using the stone. They sent it off to Bingley and used it to build the lock cottage. The house you can see today is like a giant jigsaw, and I dare say if you pulled it down and reordered the stones, you could still spell out the name Leeds and Liverpool Canal

Out in the countryside, the Leeds & Liverpool sweeps round the low hills in a series of extravagant curves.

Company. It is no surprise to find he knows so much about this length of canal, for he has worked here all his life – in fact, he told me he'd been at work for twenty years before he even so much as saw another length of canal. His was a small world, but he knew it intimately. He had the movement of the seasons to provide variety. In winter there was ice breaking, when the old boat was brought out and rocked up and down on the ice, to the delight of any small boys who could wangle a place on board. In summer there was water conservation to worry about. The lock keeper had a heavy responsibility for regulating traffic in order to save water, but the boatmen simply wanted to get on as quickly as possible. It became a battle of wits. One lock keeper rigged up a warning bell that sounded if any boatman tried to sneak through after dark. The boatmen won that one: they hired out local lads to get up every hour on the hour to open the gates and ring the bell. A few sleepless nights with not a boat in sight and the bell came down. No doubt he has known hard times, but he never speaks of them.

Bingley Five is followed by Bingley Three, and although Shipley and Bradford are just around the corner, the canal takes you through a pleasant wooded cutting, down by the River Aire. The scene opens out again at Hirst lock, where we were literally cheered on our way by a crowd of spectators, who had just left a nearby football match. Judging by their enthusiasm, the home team won. It was a pleasant overture to a pleasant theme, for we were just running into Saltaire, a remarkable settlement on the edge of Bradford. Ask any local for a one-word description of Bradford buildings, and he'll probably come up with something unprintable or the word 'black'. But there's no black at Saltaire, no hint of grime. It is almost pure white. And the architecture! In this part of the world, architecture tends to come either in unwieldy chunks, solid mills and long terraces, or in grandiose Gothic. Not at Saltaire. Here the style is all Italian – even the mill has a Florentine touch.

Saltaire was the brain child of Sir Titus Salt, manufacturer of mohair and the very model of the Victorian self-made man. In 1848 and 1849 he had been the mayor of Bradford, a town that was notorious for its spread of filthy streets of back-to-back houses, the work of unfettered speculators. Salt determined to add his own portion to Bradford, and to teach 'an important and practical lesson to the mother town'. His town was to be smoke free. The houses were not to be crammed together, but set out in wide streets and squares. There was to be a market, a school, a hospital, alms houses, bath houses, a church and a park down by the river where the workers from Salt's huge factory could take a leisurely stroll under the bronze eye of their benefactor on his pedestal overlooking the lawns and walks. Saltaire was to have everything a community should have, and nothing a community should not have. Top of the list of 'should nots' came the demon drink, and even today there is still no pub in Saltaire. The new houses, though, are remarkably large by nineteenth-century working-class standards, and show a surprising range of variation in their finer detailing. The town was begun in 1853, and people came to look, to admire and ultimately to ignore. Bradford went on stuffing its inhabitants into grim terraces. Saltaire continued to thrive and prosper, but found no imitators. It remained an oasis of white in a desert of grime.

The canal now forms the centre of a green belt as it threads through the heavily industrialized area that fills up most of the space between Bradford and Leeds. At Radley, we came upon something which is a commonplace on the more southerly canals, a small floating community. It's surprising not to find more, for the wide boats of the Leeds and Liverpool, fourteen foot in the beam, give nearly twice as much living space as the narrow boats of the Midlands. Admittedly, there is not the same housing shortage here as there is further south. There is no lack of semi-derelict properties which would have been snapped up and done up in other areas. The dead houses seem to go

Skipton was a quiet market town, but the arrival of the canal acted as a spur to industrial development.

with the dead mills. Industry and commerce are shifting away from their old centres.

Leeds comes upon you gradually. The wide Aire valley gives you a good view of the city, piled up on its hill. Familiar landmarks come up over the horizon, including the white tower of the University where I happily misspent my undergraduate youth. From a distance, Leeds seems predominantly Victorian, but there are plenty of reminders of an earlier foundation. At Kirkstall, we passed the blackened ruins of the twelfth-century Cistercian abbey. It is a remarkable building which deserves to be better known and probably would be, given a more romantic setting. Darkened by soot and sadly forlorn, it huddles into the space left between river and railway.

This is the tallest and one of the finest of the great medieval abbeys, built all of a piece in one period. Lack of popularity can bring compensations, though. If you go to Tintern, say, you'll almost certainly find the place crowded with visitors. At Kirkstall, you'll as likely as not have the place to yourself. Alone in the great nave, the noise of distant trains no more disturbing than the sound of motor coach and car, you can capture the sense of awe that the builders intended you should feel when faced with a majestic structure built for no 'practical' purpose. The abbey is less a building for the use of men than the expression of an ideal.

If the sight of the ruined abbey invokes vague mystical yearnings, then the sight and smell of the Mackeson brewery soon dispels them and you are into Leeds proper. We moored close to the heart of the city, under the shadow of the high railway embankment that leads to the terminus at City Station. I don't suppose I'd really looked at the city very closely since those undergraduate days of twenty years ago and my reactions were certainly mixed. Some things, of course, had changed out of all recognition. There are no trams clanking through Leeds any more, no stops while the conductor gets out the long bamboo pole to reconnect the power when things come adrift. There are other, more subtle, differences. I came out into the square in front of City Station and found all the main features that I remembered were there but small changes had shifted the emphasis. It was at once familiar and strange. The Black Prince still sits on his horse and points dramatically away at nothing in particular. But the naked ladies who surround him, incongruous on such a draughty site, now seem lost among the new complex traffic scheme. Old buildings have found new uses. The corner cinema is a bingo hall, and the old news cinema, where you could while away an hour with Tom and Jerry and Pluto

The Springs
Branch of the
Leeds & Liverpool
was built to serve
local quarries
and passes right
beneath the walls of
the castle.

while you waited for your train, now has soft porn. The whole square seems to have been downgraded: no longer an imposing, open space, but marked off by railings into tight little areas – here you may walk, here you may drive. It is all very practical, no doubt, but it has broken up the space and lessened its impact.

Leeds seems to be in the balance. Some parts are superb, others appalling. You just cannot tell which way the scale is going to tip. The appalling parts are plain enough for anyone to see, so let's forget about them and look at what is really good and vital in the city. The obvious starting point is the pedestrianized shopping area, an ugly phrase to describe a very attractive scheme. What distinguishes the Leeds scheme from similar schemes in other cities is that this is not a custom-built area, but an adaptation of existing shopping streets. Now the shopper can wander comfortably through the rows of Victorian shops and appreciate the quality of the past – the watchmaker with his splendidly ornate sign and his *Tempus Fugit* reminder of impermanence, the solid commercial buildings in that heavy classical style intended to impress the visitor with a sense of reliable worthiness. Best of all the refurbished areas are the superb Victorian arcades, such as Thornton Arcade, rich with cast-iron tracery and glass, domes and pilasters, colonnades and bright paintings. Victorian they may be, but they remind us that Leeds is built up around the old medieval pattern of alleys and courts. And there are the civic buildings: the town hall by Brodrick, very handsome on its high plinth, but mistakenly cleaned so that instead of being a sombre black it is now a dingy grey. There's the corn exchange, a rotunda that's finding a new use as a covered market – that's a great favourite of mine. Yes, there are lots of good things here, but I cannot help noticing, too, that there has been a decline in the quality of city life, a decline, certainly not limited to Leeds, which has been going on for a long time. It is not something you are aware of, walking around daytime Leeds: it is at night when the city empties, when the late editions blow through the deserted streets, that you feel it. The crowds have gone because there is not enough to keep them or draw them back. It is a chicken and egg situation: do the crowds leave because there are no attractions, or do the attractions close because there are no crowds? When I was a schoolboy I used to go and hear the old Yorkshire Symphony Orchestra at Leeds Town Hall. The orchestra is no more – just part of the life of the city that died away. This decline has been paralleled by the growing inhumanity of the city centre, the replacement of buildings that kept a human scale by the bland, impersonal statements of the 'internationally' styled blocks.

But for all the uneasiness, I don't feel that Leeds has slipped as far as some places. The threat has been recognized. Good luck to the place and its lively, robust heritage. Long may it be with us. I remember bemoaning the decline of Leeds in a pub and my companion, an old Yorkshireman, got quite angry. 'Headingley's still here, ain't it? They've still got Yorkshiremen playing for t'county. That's what bloody matters. Not some daft buildings.' He could be right at that. If changes go wrong, there are people around to put things right. They had the infernal cheek recently to remove part of Yorkshire and put it into Lancashire. The county cricket authority promptly sent out a note stating quite firmly that boundary committees could do what they liked, but the county selectors would take no notice. It was all still Yorkshire to them. Very reassuring that was, and there's still enough of that sort of attitude around in Leeds to make the future seem at least hopeful.

CHAPTER 9

Tom Pudding Land

Leeds marked a real turning point in our journey. We came in on the canal but went out on the river navigation. For the first time, we were about to travel waterways where trade was not just a distant, romantic memory. You feel the difference at once, as you move out on to the wide, deep waters. The speed of the boat picks up. It is like changing the old family banger for a new sports car. All around us were the signs of a thriving commercial life, and reminders of just how important river traffic was in the creation of the early commercial centres. Out on the river, warehouses and wharves are still in use, and even the steam cranes, used for unloading coal at the Co-op wharf, were working until a year or so ago. Locks are modern, with traffic lights to control the movement of boats, and instead of the usual sensation of trying to get a big boat into a small lock, you suddenly feel you are in a very small boat all but lost in the lock chamber. After two weeks of sweating over heavy gates and obstinate paddle gear it is undeniably pleasant to put your feet up, as it were, while the man in the control cabin presses a few buttons to work the whole lot.

Our view of industry so far had mostly been of the old and decaying, which is what you might expect to find along a transport route that is itself old, if not actually decaying. There is no longer a rush to site a factory by the cut. This is understandable, but it does mean that the canal traveller begins to wonder if everything is not running down, collapsing around us. Now that we were out on the broad commercial waterway we began to see evidence of the new industrial life. The old clothing industry from which Leeds once gained its prosperity is pushed further and further into the background, while the engineering works and chemical plants spread out over acres of ground. But these new industries have brought new problems with them – heavy transport, the need for more and more land, waste, pollution. The Aire and Calder pierces the industrial waste land, flat, marked only by the man-made heaps of spoil. It is a scene of devastation, a nightmare landscape. Nothing grows here. Not even the scavenger birds hover. There is only dust whipped up by the wind. The brief glimpses of apparently natural ponds and pools are deceptive for they, too, are part of the wilderness, mining flashes or chemical dumps. This is the landscape we create as we create our wealth.

Waste is the most obvious problem here, but transport does not lag so very far behind. You do not need to be any kind of a genius to see that our waterways are ludicrously underused. But aren't the waterways simply boring, old-fashioned things that can be pensioned off in these days of motorways and air travel? Try telling that to the French, the Dutch or the Germans, whose waterways have never been busier. I am not suggesting that we can go back to sending goods on the narrow canals, but when you see the facilities available on these broad waterways, it seems nonsense not to make use of them. Forget all romantic ideas about quiet boats chugging through unspoilt countryside; forget about the waterways being out of date, and look at the facts.

Point number one: in terms of fuel consumption, the waterways are far and away the most efficient means of moving goods that we have. Figures produced by the American Oak Ridge National Laboratory gave fuel use for waterways as 250 ton miles per gallon (that is, you can take 250 tons for one mile on one gallon of fuel). That compares with a figure of 200 ton miles per gallon for the railways, a mere 58 for roads and a miserable 3.7 for the airways. The only method of moving goods that came out as more efficient was the pipe line. Since then, B.W.B. have done their own survey and found that efficiency on the water goes up quite steeply with an increased load, reaching 368 ton miles per gallon with a load of 700 tons. Or put it another way, you need at least five times as much fuel to shift a load by road as you do by water. Now that is not unimpressive in these days of high and rising fuel costs.

At Leeds, the Leeds & Liverpool joins the Aire & Calder Navigation, which was still carrying commercial traffic.

Water transport is cheap, but is it practical? You only have to look at this part of the world to see the sort of goods that could be carried. Any route that is lined, as is the Aire and Calder, with power stations such as the vast complex at Ferrybridge on the one hand, and collieries on the other, should not have to look too far for cargoes. And ask any motorist what he feels about following great coal lorries across the country. Then, if you look towards the end of the line, you see the port of Hull, with promises of a busy export trade. And that brings us to the most hopeful, yet saddest, tale of the waterways in recent years – the BACAT story, BACAT is not, as it may sound, a new card game. The initials stand for Barge Aboard Catamaran. The system is very simple. Take ten barges, each able to carry 140 tons, and three 370-ton barges. Load them up with containers, or whatever, at some big industrial centre on the system, move your barges by push-pull tugs along the waterway to the port where the catamaran waits. Some of your barges are now winched on to the deck of the mother ship; the rest are secured between the twin hulls. Then off goes the ship to Holland or Scandinavia, and the barges slide out ready to continue their journey. And this is no futuristic fantasy. BACAT 1 was built and put into service. Then the trouble started. Hull dockers complained that their work was being taken away, BACAT was first blacked, then withdrawn and finally sold, and the scheme seems to be at an end. Yet it surely cannot be the end. It all made too much sense and, in the long term, any scheme that promotes the use of waterways promotes the use of ports, which has to be good news for Hull.

We passed the BACAT barges moored at their wharves, then chugged our own little boat into one of those vast locks. It seemed a ludicrous waste to operate it just for us. But we did meet traffic, and very exciting it was too. We rounded a corner and there, right in front of us were the high, black bows of a motorized barge, charging up the waterway, spray flying. We hit the wake and bobbed like a cork in the tide. This busy movement of boats was a welcome diversion from the flat, dull land around us, where the wind was whipping up the dust clouds from the wide acres of ploughed fields, stripped of their protecting hedgerows. We left the Aire and Calder for what promised to be an even duller stretch of water, the New Junction Canal, five miles of dead straight waterway, with just one lock and a few swing bridges to add variety. But, oh joy, oh bliss, coming out of Sykehouse lock we saw an object like a great, black serpent wriggling along on the water towards us – a train of Tom Puddings.

A tug waits by a lock on the Aire & Calder with half of its train of Tom Puddings, waiting for the rest of the compartment boats to come through the lock.

Remarkable things, Tom Puddings: simple, but so effective. A Tom Pudding is really no more than an iron coal box, about twenty foot by sixteen foot, which can be loaded up to a maximum of 35 tons, to a draught of six foot. The Tom Puddings are linked together, with a wedge-shaped boat at the front acting as a dummy bows for this flexible ship, which is towed along by a tug. The train we met had fifteen compartments, and we kept very well out of his way. It is only courtesy to give way to commercial craft. You are just trundling along for pleasure; they have to earn their keep. It is also a sound principle of self-preservation. As the lock keeper said, later: 'They'll not stop for you. They'll have you up the bank as soon as look at you.'

The first train went off on its way, and a second began to work through the lock. It was a fascinating sight to see. The hawsers that hold the train to the tug were pulled in, so that the dummy bows came right up to the stern of the tug. Then the train was broken, and the first seven containers were taken down the lock with the tug. What I wanted to know was how they were going to get the other eight Tom Puddings in without the tug. The answer was that they filled the lock and then, with the top gates open, wound up the bottom paddles, so that the flow of water simply sucked the boats into the lock. Once down, the train was reformed to follow the first on its way to Goole, where the Tom Puddings are picked up on a hydraulic hoist and their load of coal emptied into the waiting ship.

We left the Tom Puddings and headed off towards the great cooling towers of Thorpe Marsh power station. Those towers are massive but graceful, with long sweeping curves leading the eye up towards the swaying white cap of steam that drifted like cloud over a hill top. Power stations are, visually, remarkably interesting places. The contrast between square block and curved tower can be very satisfying, but they are also rather good at optical tricks. Try counting the number of towers at a big power station. As you go past, the number seems to change all the time. The explanation is that each of the towers is identical in shape and size with its neighbour, so that with the effect of perspective, one tower can be completely hidden by another. They come and go, appear and disappear, in a most bewildering manner.

At the end of the New Junction, the original plan had been to turn east towards the Trent, but as we were slightly ahead of schedule I decided to make a detour up to Sheffield and back. Lock keepers along the way greeted news of our intentions with scepticism. 'You'll never make it,' they said, shaking their heads at the thought of such folly. One even added, ominously, 'A boat went up that way last week.

We've not seen him since.' But, hardy adventurers that we were, we decided to brave the worst that Sheffield could offer and continued on our way. *En route* for Doncaster we tagged on behind a barge loaded with silica for Rotherham. The steerer leaned out of his cabin and cheerily waved us on past him. That was all very sociable of him, but as soon as we came abreast, we were held in his wash, and not only did we stop going past but, as I discovered when I cut the engine back again to idle, we couldn't go any slower either. We were stuck, side by side, and the bloke on the barge thought it was the funniest thing he'd seen for years. I stopped finding the situation funny round about the time I saw a bridge ahead which looked considerably narrower than our combined width. I put the engine into hard reverse and at last managed to slip back behind the barge. It was my first and last attempt at barge racing. I do not recommend it.

We stopped for the night in the quiet backwater at Strawberry Island, Doncaster, where we received the friendliest possible greeting from the local boat club. Doncaster seen from the water has little to recommend it, but once you get away from the town there are some delightful surprises waiting up ahead. Beyond the new viaduct that carries the A1 is a lovely valley, flanked by steep wooded slopes, beyond which the village of Sprotbrough lurks, largely unseen. They say Sir Walter Scott wrote part of *Ivanhoe* here, and you certainly could not ask for a better setting in which to let your imagination fill with romantic images. It seems as far removed from towns and industries as the upper Avon. But it was only an interlude. This is a busy commercial waterway, and one which displays to perfection the idiocy of current policy – or rather, lack of policy -towards waterways. At Sprotbrough lock we met a tug bringing three big barges down from Rotherham. The lock here is manually operated and, comparatively speaking, small. This meant that only one barge at a time could be fitted in. The tug takes one down, then waits. The second barge has to be sucked in, taken down and collected by the tug. Then the whole business is repeated for the third. It is ludicrously inefficient and time-wasting. In 1973 the Waterways Board put forward a plan to modernize the Sheffield and South Yorkshire at a cost of £3.5 million. It was rejected as too expensive. Three and a half million! The road builders spend that much before breakfast.

Not everyone, however, is in favour of mechanizing locks. The lock keeper at Sprotbrough isn't, for a start, and he has his own macabre reasons. He is a spry sixty-year-old who, with a certain amount of glee, told of his younger colleagues dropping dead all around him. I must confess I had never thought of lock keeping as an especially dangerous occupation, but as the list of fatalities stretched on and on, I began to think they'd all have done better to take up something more sensible, like test parachuting or lion taming. And it was all accounted for, he said, by the change to pushbutton operation. The poor lock keepers got fat and lazy, and then came the heart attack. Our busy sexagenarian seemed to have little cause to worry.

The rural idyll was brief. At Conisbrough industry is back with a vengeance. A vast limestone quarry quite overwhelms the lovely Don valley, and in and around the works the dust flies to settle palely over the surrounding area. Trees stand as dully grey as fossils, the air is thick with the flying dust. It is a dead, unwelcoming land. We write on our maps now 'Here be Industry' much as we used to write 'Here be Dragons' a few hundred years ago. Conisbrough Castle, a fine imposing building, stands as a reminder that this area once had a quite different character, was once as far removed from the noise and the dirt as any Kent village.

Conisbrough does boast one very grand industrial monument – its great railway viaduct. Fourteen arches of blue engineering brick carry the track towards the central girder over the water, and another fourteen carry it away again on the other side. It is high and impressive, and the tapering columns, which exaggerate the perspective effect, make it seem even higher and more impressive. The builders went to a lot of trouble at Conisbrough to make sure that the effect of grandeur was not lost in poor detail. There is a dentilled cornice below the top of the parapet, and each arch is emphasized by a course of rounded bricks that follow the line of the curve. It is all done superbly well. The irony is that it no longer has any useful function to perform. The railway is gone; the trains no longer run. How astonished the railway engineers would have been if they could see that their viaduct is reduced to the status of an antiquity, to be looked at and admired, while the old waterway they so confidently bridged still carries on with its freight trade.

As you get closer to Rotherham and Sheffield, the landscape becomes again the landscape of industry. It is a place where man's works overpower nature, even, at times, obliterate it. Thrybergh Bar Mill, for example, is a truly vast building, more than a quarter of a mile long: just a blank wall, no windows, no spaces, not a hint of embellishment. No one could ever call it beautiful but, by God, it's impressive. It impresses in the way that Hadrian's Wall impresses. The thing itself is not beautiful, not even picturesque, but it is very, very big. It is what it is, a box to keep a strip rolling mill out of the weather. That and nothing more. It's a good job it is so big, really, for otherwise we would just remark on its ugliness. Size has its own virtue. Yet even here the country creeps in. Tucked in between the steel mill and a chemical works, surrounded by the Yorkshire Alps, those soaring hills of spoil, is a smallholding where not an inch of space is wasted: vegetables in neat rows, a yard full of ducks and geese, hen houses, and a field of fat pink porkers. One of the pigs took it into his head to race us. Off he went full gallop, his great floppy ears lolloping up and down like a piggy Dumbo. But he never did manage to get airborne.

Coming through Rotherham, the view is dominated by the modern concrete viaduct that carries the M1, and for us that marked the approach of Tinsley locks where, we had been told, we would meet our doom. We had been warned of gates that wouldn't open, rubbish piled high in the canal, paddle gear that hadn't shifted in years. As it turned out, it was almost a disappointment. All we found were eleven locks that were a bit hard, but nowhere near impossible. We'd already met a lot worse than those in our travels. I'd swop them for Wigan any day. So there we were, all ready for an heroic struggle with a monster – but when the brave knights rode up the monster rolled over on its back and asked to have its tummy tickled. What an anti-climax.

Sheffield is still an iron and steel town and you see plenty of it on this route. There was one fascinating spot where they were breaking up scrap. Tall cranes were picking up heavy weights and dropping them down on to the metal. They were all grouped around the yard, each with its own little pit of scrap. Swing, dip, drop, swing, dip, drop.

They seemed to be moving to the design of some intricate mechanical choreography. But the real excitement comes when you go past a strip rolling mill. Through the open doors you can see the red hot bars, snaking across the floor, whipped along from roller to roller with pincers wielded by men who are as casual as if they were picking up lumps of sugar with sugar tongs at a vicarage garden party.

From the top lock it is no more than a couple of miles to the terminus at Sheffield Basin. It is a spectacular place, right in the heart of the city, that could be for the northern waterways what Gas Street once was for the Midlands. To appreciate the importance of Sheffield Basin, you have to think of it in terms of its whole setting. Across the main road is a new shopping centre, with a big covered market which, incidentally, is first class. Overlooking the site is a gigantic block of flats. They say it is the largest housing complex of its kind in Europe. Like Thrybergh Mill it impresses by sheer scale, especially at night when the walkways are lit. It looks like a cliff with caves. In daylight, at closer quarters, it has that air of dejected shabbiness that one so often finds in such projects. The newer materials don't weather; they stain. The canal basin is as remote from all this as a moon base. It is a totally enclosed area, with tall mills and warehouses, one of which stands on arches, straddling the water. These buildings are listed for preservation. While this means they may not be killed, it does not mean that anyone must strive officiously to keep them alive. Any scheme that is to make this basin into an area that will contribute something special to city life must take care to retain the feeling of enclosure. There is a practical reason. Sheffield is a notoriously windy city, and if you open up the basin, you will create a wind tunnel. And there is an aesthetic reason. If you open out, you destroy the sense of unity, the sense of a complete, separate world, a world of stone buildings and cobbled quaysides that exists all by itself in the middle of a modern city. It would be pleasant to think that a community use could be found for the buildings, as an arts centre or youth club. But whatever the use, let us hope that one lesson will be heeded. It is not single buildings that matter here, but the whole. Destroy a part, you destroy all. Remember Gas Street!

Sheffield itself has been largely rebuilt since the last war, but whatever you do to Sheffield you can never quite change a character that owes as much to nature as to man. The city starts in the narrow river valley, then climbs the steep hillside, and where the city ends the moor begins. With that sort of geography, you either have to fit in as best you can or risk looking silly and pretentious. Some of the off-the-peg glass and concrete boxes in the centre look just that. Not much of old Sheffield

Thorpeness
power station on
the Sheffield &
South Yorkshire.

remains, though there is a fine Georgian square in the centre, Paradise Square, and as you move outwards you find solid stone houses that seem absolutely right for the city. Of the new, I liked the market best, although it is a bit compartmentalized. I suppose, however, there is a good case for keeping the fishmongers, for example, all in the one area. It's lively, offers good value, and, most important, it offers variety. It still has room for the tripe stall. But it's *where* it is more than *what* it is that makes Sheffield a pleasure to visit.

We left the city and retraced our steps until we were past the end of the New Junction where we had turned off three days before, and then we were in new territory. Not, however, into country that inspires any great affection in me. This is a flat land, as flat as Holland but considerably less interesting. In Holland you have the constant interruptions of little farms, hamlets, towns. From miles away you can see the church towers and, of course, the windmills. Here you have power stations and pitheads and not very many of those. Yet there are similarities with Holland's landscape for this, too, is land won for man by drainage. Impressive work it must once have been, but now there are only the long, straight lines of the dykes – and the long, straight line of the canal. Once you leave Bramwith Junction and go down Bramwith lock, monotony sets in. There is Thorne lock, a succession of swing bridges, and that's it. Even the canal traffic offered little to enthuse over. For miles we trekked after a tanker carrying what the lock keeper euphemistically described as 'effluent'. From the aroma that wafted down the wind, it was very obvious just what sort of effluent it was. A grey day, a chill wind and a boat load of sewage to follow – not my idea of bliss.

On a section like this you look out for each and every interruption to relieve the boredom of a steady chunter down the middle of a dead straight canal. There's a glimpse of an otter, scuttling along the bank on absurdly short legs, then sliding gracefully into the water; a crested grebe bobs along quietly, minding its own business, then suddenly notices the barge bearing down on it and gets into a rare old panic; a flight of geese pose for the living-room wall; a kestrel is mobbed by irate gulls. There's a great white owl, batting at the air in slow motion, a skylark soaring and plummeting in incessant song, swans in flight like precursors of the supersonic age. Nature provides all the interest here, for man has created an empty land for himself: no hedgerows, no fences, just the vast fields where dust flicks in the east wind. There are a few settlements. Thorne arrives with a sudden eruption of boats at the busy boatyard. Stainforth offers something a bit more like the familiar canal scene. A row of eighteenth-century cottages face the water and there is even a canalside pub.

The main amusement on this whole length is the chance to exchange friendly chat with bridge keepers and lock keepers – mostly friendly, anyway. One complained bitterly, and not without reason, about the expert who had come to see him and had decreed that the bridge over the lock should be removed. Now, when he wants to get out of the cottage, he has to walk over the top of the lock gates, and you can imagine how easy life becomes when you only have access to the outside world by hopping over a lock gate. I listened for some time to his views on the 'know-alls from Oxford', and thought it wisest not to tell him where I'd come from.

At Keadby the canal joins the river, but before you reach the end of the line you encounter a real curiosity – a railway bridge, built skew over the canal, that slides to one side to allow water traffic through. There is only one other bridge like it anywhere in the world. Keadby itself has no very marked characteristic. There is a power station which is in use but which appears permanently deserted, a few houses and the lock leading into the Trent. Before I left on the trip I had had a call from Dave Bradford, who had ferried a number of boats up and down the tidal Trent. He volunteered his services for this part of the trip, and I was very happy to accept. I have a great respect for tidal waters and it seems to me to be foolish not to take advantage of any expert help that's going. The Trent is tidal from Keadby to Cromwell lock, forty-four miles upstream. You have to go up with the tide, joining at slack water in order to reach Cromwell before the turn. A boat like ours would have real difficulty battling against tide and current. I had no wish to anchor on the river and even less wish to find myself disappearing backwards in the general direction of the North Sea.

The end of the canal at Sheffield basin: the area has since been extensively developed.

Dave had worked out that we could leave Keadby at 7.15 in the morning, so I wandered up for a word with the lock keeper. I told him about our plans, and was more than a little startled by his reaction. '7.15! Whoever told you that?' I explained that our expert had calculated the time. '7.15? No chance. You'll not be out at 7.15.' It looked as if our plans were going to be thrown out of the window. It was not just the tide that mattered. We were limited to daylight travel since we weren't equipped with navigation lights. I asked nervously what time he thought we might get out on to the river. Still laughing at the thought of a 7.15 start, the lock keeper thought for a moment. 'You'll be lucky if you're out much before 7.30!'

That evening we wandered up towards the river. Across the water a distant glow, a reddish light surrounding the clouds of smoke and steam that rose from the steel works of Scunthorpe. It is a memorable sight, and somewhere from the back of my mind I dredged up some words by Milton, the description of the opening of the Gates of Hell in *Paradise* Lost:

> So wide they stood, and like a furnace mouth
> Cast forth rebounding smoke and ruddy flame.

There could hardly be an apter image for the inferno than those furnaces that lit the night sky.

CHAPTER 10

Burton on Trent

A magical morning. Just after half past seven the lock gates opened and we slipped out under the stern of an anchored coaster on to the broad waters of the Trent. We headed straight out to the wide yellow disc of the sun, before swinging into the tide and away towards the dark silhouette of the bridge. There was a raw, cold wind so that it seemed more like November than April, but the boat shot smoothly through the water, parting the white wisps of mist that hovered over the surface. The Trent, like all tidal waters, can change its mood quickly and dramatically, but that morning we found it at its gentlest, and the precautionary anchor stayed in its locker. It was as peaceful as an outing on the Isis.

The river runs between high flood banks, which effectively cut off the view of the surrounding land. Only the drainage ditches and the settlements that creep up to the backs of the banks provide variety. But it really does not matter, for there is such delight in the river itself. The pale sun bounces on the water, fragmenting in the swirl of the wake. And there is a kind of tension in the travelling, for you have to remind yourself that the river is a potential danger, and keep a close eye on your navigation. You keep an eye open, too, for other craft, which are liable to be a good deal bigger and very much faster than your own boat.

There are two places you can leave the river – bolt holes if you need them. The first is West Stockwith Basin which marks the beginning of the Chesterfield Canal. There was no time to stop, which was rather a pity, as I'd have liked to renew an old acquaintance. Last time I came this way, I was wandering around the village of West Stockwith, down by the River Idle, when I saw something that looked remarkably like a steam-engine house. Now that was not something I'd expected to see in this part of the world, so I went for a closer look. It obviously was an engine house and it was attached to something that appeared to be a mill. While I was puzzling over just what it might be, a woman came out from the mill house. She not only told me the story of the mill, but also told me the story of her family, of West Stockwith and the Trent and anything else I cared to know about. The mill turned out to be a flax mill, long disused. The family that lived there had been butchers, and the old building had served as a slaughter-house. She took me on a tour and showed me the hole in the wall through which the cattle used to stick their heads for father to pole-axe them. She remembers the slaughter-house with affection. As a child, she told me, it used to be a treat to have a ride on the carcase as it was winched through for carving. It was an even bigger treat to be allowed to jump up and down on it to help pump out the blood.

Past Stockwith the river becomes rather more winding in its course, and we rounded one of those big bends to be confronted by a pair of coasters coming down from Gainsborough on the rising tide. They may have been quite small by merchant shipping standards, but they looked like giants to me. The tall bows sliced the water and I swung our boat wide, then headed it back in towards the wash. We bounced furiously in the wake, and settled down again. The captain of the second boat leaned out from the edge of the bridge and shouted down to ask if there were any more boats behind us – captain-to-captain conversation.

Gainsborough has very much the air of the seaport about it. Docks and warehouses, the quayside buildings, all look as though they ought to be facing out towards the ocean. These days, though, the whole view is dominated by the huge Spillers mill, and even when you get through the town the mill maintains its dominance as you twist and turn with the river. It's amazing how it keeps popping up into view, to stern, to either side and once, rather startlingly, straight ahead again.

Villages appear, peep briefly over the bank, and then go again. It is rather like travelling by car. The extra bit of speed doesn't seem to allow you quite enough time to take things in, and those coasters acted as a reminder that it is unwise to spend too much time staring at the scenery. Torksey marks the opening of the Foss Dyke and the last of the bolt holes before Cromwell. It comes and goes quickly by. The absence of settlement along the river goes with the absence of bridges. The Trent is a resolute divider of the land. At Dunham, however, someone had the sense to capitalize on the lack and built a toll bridge. You still have to pay to get across. Gradually, though, the scenery changes. The dead flatness begins to shift into a steady undulation of hill and hollow. The occasional windmill adds a little variety, though I am always amazed there are not more in such a wind-swept land.

Shortly after two o'clock we reached Cromwell lock, having made such good time that we had actually outpaced the tide, travelling the last few miles on the tail end of the ebb. The tidal waters were behind us. The river at once seemed to take on a new character now that it was its own master, unaffected by the sea. Villages and towns crept out from behind cover, showing some very handsome faces to the

Early morning sun at Keadby by the lock that leads out into the tidal River Trent.

world, and none handsomer than at North Muskham, which boasts an unusually fine parish church with large clerestory windows. Two last wiggles – the Trent has moved around a good deal over the centuries and has gained a few convolutions in the process – and we were at Newark Nether lock, a splendid name that makes you think back to medieval times. Through the lock into Newark cut, and the end of the day's travel was in sight. The Trent, which can be quite fearsome, had turned out to be in soporific mood, and we felt rather smug and self-congratulatory as we moved into the moorings at the town wharf. Then there was the most appalling crunch and clatter of metal. It sounded as though the prop was being churned to small pieces. Hastily we shut off the engine and got the weed-hatch off to inspect the damage. To our great relief, the prop was intact. And that was a miracle, for a metal rod was sticking out of the wharf wall, below the waterline, We had hit the rod, but by great good fortune it had ridden up over the top of the rudder and jammed there. No harm done, if you don't count heart failure among the crew.

Newark: castle, church, breweries, market, port, not necessarily in that order. It is a town with a multiplicity of activities that give it a multiplicity of aspects. We came in under the comparatively new A1 bypass bridge, and how much Newark has benefited from the loss of those long, grinding queues of traffic in the town centre. Coming in by water, you start with the imposing brick maltings and breweries. These buildings always seem to me to be full of character, and I don't think it's just an association of ideas. In fact they provide very powerful shapes, their high pyramid roofs over the malting kilns making for a strong, geometric pattern on the skyline. These are purely functional buildings, with forms and textures derived from the needs of the works. So you find brick and stone used for the main structures but this is offset by the wooden covers over the sack hoists. It is all very satisfying. At the centre of the town overlooking the cut is Newark Castle, an imposing facade with a lovely oriel window thrust out over the water. Alas, facade is all it is, for the rest has gone, knocked down by Cromwell when the long Civil War siege of the town finally came to a conclusion.

Nothing in Newark, though, can really compete with the magnificence of the parish church of St Mary Magdalene. The spire reaches up 252 feet, demanding attention. No matter how you approach Newark, your eye is drawn by that insistent exclamation mark on the skyline. You would be well advised to go and see what all the excitement is about, for beneath that spire is one of the most beautiful, and certainly one of the grandest, parish churches in the land. Like so many large churches, it has grown over the centuries, so that to walk around the building is to get a quick lesson in architecture. The oldest part of the building dates back to the twelfth century, but not a great deal of the Norman church remains, and what does remain is mostly out of sight in the crypt. The rest is splendidly in view. You have to start with that tower and spire, so beautifully proportioned, so perfectly balanced. Yet the Early English tower was built in 1230 and that fine octagonal spire was not added until a full century later. Bits kept being added to the building. The south aisle was begun in the fourteenth century in the then popular Decorated style. But that great scourge, the Black Death, came to Newark and fifty years passed before work was resumed. By that time fashion had changed, and the aisle was finished off in the new Perpendicular style. The chancel came in 1498, and so the story continues. Yet look around, and it is not the differences you notice, but the astonishing unity.

The church building is magnificent, but what makes it something more than a grand, rhetorical statement in stone is the wealth of fine detail. Some of the details have been added by known craftsmen, others by anonymous workers. A huge building is always in danger of seeming rather impersonal, and these carvings and the stained glass restore to it a sense of the individual. Devil and saint live in close proximity in the medieval church, but the old craftsmen who were responsible for the carving found the grotesque devils more fun. The pious, bland saints inside are pallid creatures when set against the gargoyles that squint and leer down at you from the roof. The wooden screen and misericords in the chancel were all the work of the great York carver, Thomas Drewserd, who, like all the greatest carvers in wood, kept the organic, sensuous feel of the raw material alive in his work. But of all the works that craftsmen have wrought in this church none are more moving than the rich, stained-glass windows, vibrant and reverberating with intense blues and reds and golds.

Castle and church were the focal points of medieval Newark, but much of the rest of the medieval town has gone, removed by those most ruthless of property developers, the Georgians. They did, however, preserve much of the original pattern of the town, so that there is still a labyrinth of narrow streets and alleys, giving constantly changing views. And they left one fine, fourteenth-century timbered inn, the White Hart. At the centre of the complex web is the market square with the Town Hall at one end, an elegant Palladian building of 1773, which has been spared the indignity suffered by another nearby classical building of being turned into a bingo hall. And there is one other focus at Newark, the river, lined by some really impressive warehouses. Seen from the river, Newark is a town of roofs. They seem to tumble down the slope towards the water, a rich pattern of warm colour and texture, brick, tile and slate. They were almost the last sight we had of the town when, on the Sunday, we were back on the water with a cold wind blowing. But we still had plenty of company – rowing boat, sailing boat, little puttering motor boat and the desperately unstable-looking modern skiff that flicks over the water like that busy little insect, the water boatman. People enjoy rivers, and there were lots of people out strolling along the banks. You leave Newark much as you enter it, past the buildings of old industry, then you are out of the cut and into the windings of the river itself. Newark steeple continues to hold the skyline until that role is taken over by Staythorpe power station. Power stations do tend to dominate this river and, indeed, further on at Trent Port, a grandiose name for a very small jetty, the spectator has the dubious pleasure of being able to see three of them at the same time. At Staythorpe the authorities have acknowledged their debt to the river and have placed a very pleasant piece of sculpture on the bank – a nice friendly touch.

The river becomes progressively more attractive. At Farndon there is a delightful riverside village and the Brittania, an equally delightful riverside pub: certainly it lured me, but I resisted temptation and sailed on past. I regretted that later, for it turned out to be the last pubbish pub we were to meet before Nottingham. The ferry boat inn rules here, too big for intimacy and comfort, old-fashioned rather than old-world.

Unexpectedly and rather intimidating large companions on the Trent.

They seem to belong in the world of flappers and cocktails, Ben Travers farces and men in white flannel trousers. They do not entice; the river does. The left bank rises in high bluffs of reddish soil where the sandstone occasionally breaks through the thick covering of trees, while to the right are rich green meadows pied with daisies. Then there are locks with universally friendly lock keepers and yet more boats: sailing boats by the fleet and even water skiers, shimmering like eels in their glossy, black wet suits. So the day passed cheerfully enough and we moored for the night by the elegant cast-iron span of the Trent Bridge in Nottingham, bright with fresh paint. It is a bridge that would not disgrace the Seine, but then if it was in Paris it would not have a County Cricket ground at one end and a good, honest boozer at the other.

A man at Radio Nottingham told me that Nottingham in the seventies was desperately trying to correct the awful blunders made in the sixties. It does not take very long to discover the mistakes. There are two obviously important centres in Nottingham, the castle on its high rock and the market square. In the sixties the authorities decided to open up the city to the motor car. It was the most brutal kind of municipal surgery, performed without the benefit of anaesthetic. A great gash was made between the two centres, cutting them off from each other, severing the old streets. Surgery complete, the monstrous scar that was left was named Maid Marian Way – which shows someone had a sense of humour. But these latter-day Robin Hoods reversed the old fable. They stole the city from the poor citizens, and handed it over to the rich developers. Development was simply allowed to run rampant, and bad was made worse by the crushingly dull blocks that were set up along the new route.

Now, rather belatedly, the mistakes have been recognized. The cars still have their throughway, but they have been banished from the area around the market square. Streets have been paved and, as so often happens when people have the chance to stand and stare without running the risk of being run over, a lot of charm is being revealed. I don't think anyone would claim that Nottingham has any great wealth of architecture, but it is rediscovering its identity – and creating a new one.

The area around the castle still shows something of the character of an older Nottingham, a mixture of Georgian and Elizabethan. Sadly, too many buildings have been left stranded by that Maid Marian Way. Half - timbered houses look gloomily down on the concrete wilderness. But here is the Trip to Jerusalem, a pub which makes the not undisputed claim to be the oldest in Britain. It is a fascinating little place, built into the castle rock itself, the sort of place one might expect to find sinking

under the weight of plastic souvenirs and appalling names (I did see a Friar Tuck Shop in the town). But, bless it, this is just a good pub with good ale where one can sit by a big coal fire for a pint and a chat.

All these different aspects of Nottingham have very little to do with the route we followed through the city, as we left the wide river for the narrow Beeston Canal. It turned out to be one of those familiar murky waterways creeping past the arse end of industry. What we saw from the boat were the oldest factories, often sulking behind high walls, though there was one reminder of the most famous of all the canal carrying companies when we reached the wharf where Fellows, Morton and Clayton once ran their fleet of narrow boats. It is a reminder that Nottingham was once a town of heavy industry, notorious for the worst slums in Britain. The Nottingham courtyards were worse than anything that Manchester or the Glasgow Gorbals could produce. And it is still an industrial city. Once you're clear of the Victorian terraces of Beeston – which are by no means a gloomy sight – you meet the new

A pleasant mooring at the end of the tidal river beside the castle at Newark.

industrial estates, which turn out to be a very pleasant surprise. The new buildings are good, clean and honest and though they have few frills, they do provide rich surfaces and a good deal of variety, far more than you get in most office developments. In fact, from a purely visual point of view, you could make out a very good case for banishing the offices to the outer suburbs and bringing the factories into the centre. They'd be a lot more exciting to look at.

Once you leave the canal and return to the river, you meet a strange scene. All along the river bank a kind of shanty town has grown up, a weird colony of do-it-yourself housing. Most of the buildings are wooden and owe nothing whatsoever to the formal rules of architecture. People have simply come along and banged a lot of planks together to resemble an ideal suburban Mon Repos or a miniature Swiss chalet. It is all very personal, a kind of folk art, very like garden sheds on allotments and pigeon lofts, little triumphs of ingenuity over circumstance.

We passed a watery crossroads, where the Erewash Canal leads off to the north and the Soar Navigation goes away to the south, then came out under the M1, to be faced quite suddenly by the unmistakable outlines of canal lock and canal bridge. The river journey was over, and we were back with the old, familiar world of the canals.

The old Fellows, Morton & Clayton warehouse in Nottingham.

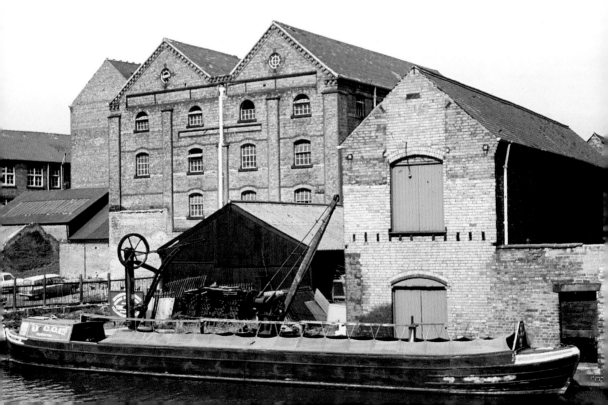

CHAPTER 11

Old Towns

Much as I enjoyed my journey down the Trent, I was more than delighted to be back on the canal. Not that I had much time to appreciate the joys of canal travel on that day: we had scarcely begun to travel down the Trent and Mersey before we reached Shardlow where we planned to stop for the night.

Shardlow is very much a canal town, for it was the canal that called it into being. In the middle of the eighteenth century there was nothing here but a few scattered farms. Then the Trent and Mersey Canal was planned, and it was inevitable that somewhere near the spot where canal and river were to meet, a new inland port would appear. River boats would have to shift their cargoes to canal boats, and vice versa, so warehouses would have to be built. The terminus became the natural nucleus for a small settlement. There were homes for the warehousemen and wharfingers, offices for administrators. Then, once the place started to grow, shops were needed and inns for visiting traders and still more homes for those who provided the different services. Shardlow was a Georgian new town, a creature of its age.

Coming into Shardlow the commercial buildings make the strongest impression, not just because of their size but because of the wealth of interesting detail. Here a warehouse has little semicircular windows with iron tracery, while another has a rounded corner with corbelled overhang, built that way to make maximum use of space, and rounded off at ground level to avoid damage from the busy traffic of carts and waggons. Further along is Trent Mill, the best known of the Shardlow buildings, built over a wide arch where boats once floated ready for loading, out of the way of wind and rain. Around these are the houses, and how well the different elements of Shardlow fit together, mill and warehouse blending as a coherent whole. The overall scale of the buildings may be quite different, but they are all built of the same warm brick and the details, such as doors and windows, bear a very close family resemblance. There used to be a lot more of Georgian Shardlow, but the last few years have seen much destruction. Old mill buildings have gone, to be replaced by new houses. Hoardings proudly assert the virtues of a canal view, a fact that not so long ago would have been discreetly overlooked. Real canal Georgian has gone; pseudo canal Georgian has come in.

Shardlow only developed when the Trent & Mersey Canal arrived, hence the large number of handsome Georgian houses.

Needless to say, the inland port provided plenty of customers for the local pubs, and there are still two by the canal. We visited the New Inn. In this context, the name 'new' generally means that the inn was new when the canal was new; genuinely new inns carry names like Ye Olde Canale Inne. There we were greeted by a luxuriantly bewhiskered landlord who served us up with moderately priced bread and cheese, offering a choice of a whole range from good French to rare old Stilton.

The canal lies along the bottom of the Trent valley, a rich river plain of arable and pasture land, complete with the inevitable Trent power stations. It is a flat land that you would see at its best on a pleasant, calm day. It was our misfortune to be there on a day when the wind whipped over the land with what seemed near-hurricane ferocity; the sort of wind that slices to the bone no matter how you pile on the clothing. You begin really to hate a wind like that after a while, and you appreciate how men used to think of such forces as gods, each with their own characteristic temperaments. I could imagine a wind god, all right, and if I'd known the appropriate incantation to appease him I'd have tried it out. As it was, he just kept on howling, and it seemed he'd never stop.

You get broad locks here, with little stubby gates. They look almost insignificant after the great barge and river locks, but don't be fooled. They're vicious little things, those Trent and Mersey locks, and if you don't want to be thrown from side to side or risk a flooding, then it is advisable to use the ropes to hold the boat in place, and the best way to do that is to slip the stern line round the edge of the gate recess, which stops the boat from moving forwards. It was the lock keeper who recommended that particular method. We chatted about the current water restrictions and he reckoned canal users had brought them down on their own heads, by simply not thinking about saving water, by not sharing locks, by not closing paddles. He could well be right. Perhaps this year, though, the lesson will go home.

A short way from the canal is the railway, a familiar companion, for the sort of level ground the canal engineers hunted out was just the sort of ground the railwaymen were looking for. Although it is usually quite near, you see very little of the railway. It appears briefly over a bridge, then it is off again. But on this route the railway makes its own level, banging across the valley on an embankment, ruling a division over the land. It is certainly intrusive, but it has its compensations. Where the bank cuts off the view, gaps for bridges suddenly open it out again. And the bridges themselves are interesting – a good stone bridge here, quite an elaborate cast-iron bridge there.

It is hard to think of a more English scene than that offered by the Trent valley with its broad, lush meadows studded with grazing cattle, the little villages in which the church tower is the only prominent landmark. Yet if you stop near Weston and eavesdrop on the local farm workers, you'll hear some very un-English conversation. The topics are those you'll hear from any farmers – the miseries of the weather, the price of feedstuffs – but the language is the language of the Ukraine. Here is an expatriate community who are keeping their old customs and language alive because, as they will tell you in imperfect English, one day things will change, one day they will go home. And in the meantime a whole new generation is growing up which has never seen the Ukraine.

At Swarkestone, we were joined by the old Derby Canal, at a junction marked by a toll house. It is at first sight rather strange to see a canal toll house built to the same pattern as the more familiar road toll houses. You can see the advantages, though, of that projecting bay front, which gives the wary collector a good, all-round view. No one was going to slip past there without paying his dues. Now the toll house, with the small warehouse and stables alongside, no longer has a job to do: no tolls to collect, no horses to feed, not even any cargoes to store. Time has simply left them stranded, fossil buildings, a tangible record of the old trading days on the Trent and Mersey.

The first major town we met along the way was Burton-on-Trent. We came into the town past one of those delightful small yards that are so much a feature of the canal scene. Horninglow wharf has the original warehouse straddling the canal, like some triumphal arch welcoming you. But it is your nose that first tells you just what sort of town you are visiting. The wind carries the smell of malt and hops, the powerful, slightly sickly smell of brewing. The canal itself scarcely penetrates the town but keeps edging out along the eastern boundary. It is the railway that cuts into the centre, a main line surrounded by a complex of sidings and branches that slice across and through the streets of Burton. But the canal does give the best view of the breweries and that, after all, is what this town is all about.

They have been brewing ale in this area for seven hundred years, since the monks of Burton Abbey first discovered that the waters of the Trent were just the stuff for a good beer. At one time any decent sized town would have had its brewery, and even the bigger estates would include brewhouses among the outbuildings. But it was the industrial revolution that turned brewing into big business. The uprooted population, crammed into the new towns, needed to have their beer

The famous old corn mill at Shardlow.

sent in from somewhere and the brewers of Burton were ideally placed to supply it. Don't get the idea that these were evil capitalists serving up drink for the sodden masses. These were philanthropists providing a public service. Beer, was, as Sellers and Yeatman would have said, A Good Thing, for the alternative was the appalling gin that really did wreak havoc among the poor of the big cities. Even John Wesley recommended his followers to drink beer, while vigorously denouncing that other pernicious evil, foreign drink that would lead them on the path to damnation – tea. Imagine a Methodist preacher thundering away from his pulpit denouncing the cup of tea, and extolling the virtues of a pint of bitter!

The great growth of urban areas in the nineteenth century did nothing to diminish the demands for more beer, and in its heyday Burton could boast more than twenty breweries. Now, sadly, the numbers have diminished to a mere half dozen, You see the familiar, well-advertised names now when you pass through Burton – Bass, Worthington, Double Diamond and the rest. The big breweries tend to be massive, brick and Victorian, built to impress. There is no reason why an industrialist should not try to produce something special in the way of buildings. He may only see the inside, but the rest of us have to look at the outside. I must say breweries do tend to come out of things rather well, but you won't find the most imposing brewery in this part of the world at all. If you really want to see just how impressive they can be, then nip up to Yorkshire and take a look at the Tadcaster Brewery. That really is something special.

Not far past Burton we came to Tatenhill lock, and the canal changed character again. The transformation that began on the previous day was now complete. Already we had moved off the river on to the broad canal, and now we were back again with the narrow lock. What is so special about a narrow canal? Tatenhill lock says it all. You come up towards a little rounded bridge, its shape accentuated by white paint on the coping. You poke the boat into the bridge hole and push the nose up towards the dark oak gates that cut off the view. The gates open and you slide snugly into the dark, dripping lock chamber, the gates close and overhead you hear the hard, staccato rattle of the gear. Then the water rushes in and you start to rise. Slowly the boat comes up the lock, and a whole new scene gradually comes into view. The first thing you see is a delightful, whitewashed lock cottage, then you're up to the new level and on your way again. At its best it is a marvellous experience, and it is at its best when all the elements gell, when the scene you rise to meet turns out to be even more attractive

The low aqueduct that carries the Trent & Mersey across the River Dove.

Tattenhill lock and bridge on the Trent & Mersey.

than you'd expected, when everything looks right and sounds right. Oh, that lovely sound of well maintained gear. It's as much a part of the canal scene as any visual feature.

The canal runs past gravel works which look rather like the traditional schoolboy's dream world. Excavated material is whipped around the big site by a complex system of conveyor belts just like a huge model railway, and one elderly gentleman has control of the whole thing. After that the A38 turned up alongside us. Being along the line of the old Roman road, it keeps a very straight course, and as we were on a very flat stretch so did we. Canal and road run side by side with not even a screen of shrub to keep them apart. You get so accustomed to being stuck away in your own private world on the canals that you feel quite vulnerable, thrust out into the open like that, with cars and lorries zipping by at what seemed a positively lunatic pace. We'd been on the go all day, and I'd had a short chat with a lock keeper, seen a man play with his conveyor railway and that was about it in the way of human contact. It was almost frightening to be suddenly faced by all this manic activity.

Then we left the road behind and approached Wychnor, and it was as though we had moved back into the world of the great English landscape painters. Wychnor itself no longer exists, but the church of St Leonard still stands, its tower picked out in the evening sun that was sending pale streaks of light across the wide meadows. Here the river put in a last appearance, and river and canal briefly joined as we went on to the little town of Alrewas. The grey morning, the vile wind were forgotten. A hazy sun turned water and sky to a mingling of soft, greyish blue, touched at the water's edge by a brilliant, metallic sheen. Along the bank, the towpath ran over a series of crisp, white trestle bridges. For just that moment all elements combined to produce something very close to perfection. In the foreground was the turning river with its little straggle of bridges; beyond that the fresh green of the water meadows and, giving point and emphasis to the horizon, the tall shapes of church tower and water mill. Then the boat rounded another curve and the magical point of balance was lost.

Alrewas itself turned out to be a village in grave danger of becoming a town. The old settlement was based on the river, which was a source of power as well as a natural boundary, and on the road which linked the river centre to the old Roman road. The church sits down by the river, a plain, unpretentious stone building, rather badly in need of a new bell. Houses group round church and church yard, and then spread out down the link road which has become the village high street. The two groups have great cohesion, and they also boast a number of individual buildings of great quality, with more than a sprinkling of timbered cottages covered in thatch, once the universal roofing material of the area. That, then, is the old village, and to the north and west development is effectively ruled out by the wide bend of the river. But the south is open, and quite large-scale development has already begun. If it goes on spreading out in the one direction, either the whole centre of the village will shift, or there will be a disastrous schism between old and new. The old centre could so easily become no more than a quaint backwater, instead of remaining what it should be, the living heart of a living community.

On the following day the wind blew again. Now it was not just cold but it brought rain driving into our faces. The sky was an uncompromising grey, and it was clearly a situation that called for emergency measures. I duly clambered into full wet-weather gear, gum boots, heavy oilskins, the lot. As soon as I emerged, doing a passable imitation of a North Sea fisherman, the rain stopped and the sun appeared. I changed back again, praying that the weather wouldn't follow suit. It didn't. We travelled with the sun on our backs all the way down to Fradley Junction, where the Trent and Mersey swings away to the north, while we turned on to the Coventry Canal, heading south.

CHAPTER 12

New Towns

At Fradley Junction we had a brief refuelling stop at the main tenance yard, which typifies the new B.W.B. look, spruce and neat in sharp black and white. Like many canal junctions, Fradley offers a Georgian microcosm. Any junction was a natural growth centre, with its yard, offices, inn and homes for the people who worked there. And because there was often nothing apart from the junction to attract newcomers, there they all remain in splendid isolation. And it really is a miniature world. The workmen's cottages look across at the very grand Junction House; rich and poor face each other across the narrow strip of water that brought them both there. I sat for a while looking at Junction House, a plain, foursquare building in red brick, the appeal of which comes in good measure from the millimetre accuracy with which the different parts stand in relation to each other. Then I turned away to continue my journey down the Coventry Canal, past a sad, disused airfield. But beyond that it was all rural landscape at its most charming as the route wandered gently among the dipping fields. Then a new housing estate appeared and crept briefly down to the water's edge – showing us its best and its worst faces. When we first met it, the street ended at a small green by the water, a well tended spot, bright with daffodils and young trees, pleasant for the house owners, pleasant for us. Further along, the houses skulked behind a high chain fence strung on ugly concrete pillars. The fence was depressing and unfriendly and the space behind it had become a rubbish dump. The usual plastic bags hung grey and limp from the trees and trash slewed down the bank.

Nearing Hopwas, the whole special character of this area, its unique dualism, was brought into sharp focus. On one side the ground heaved up in a steady rolling rhythm that ended with Hopwas Hays wood while on the other side we had a view across the valley where the river Tame flowed beneath us to Tamworth. The tower blocks stuck up on the horizon, filling the gap between cloud and earth with irregular stumps like an old crone's smile. Then at Hopwas itself we found good vernacular housing in plenty, nothing very exciting perhaps, but masterpieces of the builder's art when set against the thumping monotony of the blocks.

As we came past Fazeley Junction, where the Birmingham and Fazeley Canal comes in after its passage through Spaghetti Junction, we were pursued by a young teenage girl, bobbling along the tow-path on platform shoes like a pair of Frankenstein boots. With her long skirt and hulking great feet she looked very like one of those big-footed matchstick girls in a Lowry painting. She was trying, and failing, to run after us, so we obligingly slowed down until she had limped up to ask us where we were going. 'London', I said, since that seemed the simplest answer. Her jaw nearly touched her kneecap. 'London!' It was as if we had said we were just on our way to pick up the Holy Grail. 'Can I come too?' I politely declined the offer of her company, and chugged on, leaving her staring after creatures fortunate enough to be heading for the city of golden pavements. Poor girl, Heaven knows what she expected from the capital, but having looked across at those vistas of ugly towers, I could see why she wanted something else, a place that offered glamour and excitement. The reality of London might be very different from her media-fed image, but you couldn't blame her for wanting the change.

Across the low-arched aqueduct over the Tame, and we came up to Tamworth's massive new housing development. Here, at last, were all the qualities that one had despaired of ever seeing in such a scheme. My own predeliction for Georgian architecture must be obvious by

Fradley Junction, where the Coventry Canal leaves the Trent & Mersey. The whitewashed building is The Swan pub.

now but I am certainly not looking for new houses that slavishly copy Georgian styles. It is simply ludicrous to fill a new house with bull's-eye windows. They were never put there in the first place because people liked the style, but because that was the best the early glass makers could manage. I doubt if the Tamworth architects even thought about the eighteenth century when they designed this scheme, yet it was here that I recognized true Georgian qualities in modern building, and there's not a single period detail to be seen. Here is the same basic preoccupation with overall plan, proportion and materials, and care for detail. How often have we seen, particularly in council housing, a good house ruined by shoddy details such as cheap metal window frames. It was a delight to see, in the first group of houses we came to, that the window frames were of natural, seasoned wood. What a difference it makes, what a sense of richness it gives to the whole house. It is too early for a final judgement on the whole scheme, for it is still being built, but already a number of virtues are clearly evident. A good deal of care has gone into the planning of the area as a whole. Instead of dull regimentation, there are small groups of houses, intimate clusters. Then, coming down in scale, you can see that thought has been given to providing a good mixture of designs. I was struck by one row, where the whole terrace was enlivened by the design of the first floor windows. These alternated between the conventional window, set flat in the wall, and dormers breaking into the roof line, so that as you look down the row, the eye is led along a gently wavering line. And then the materials – the bricks may not be locally fired, but they show a richness of colour and texture. If only we'd build more places like this, there might be fewer dreamers longing for the glamour of London.

After that, by way of contrast, the canal ran slap-bang into the middle of the coal-mining region, from new estate to mining village. Amington seen from the canal is just one long, continuous terrace, but at least the houses are blessed with good, big gardens. The distant prospect may be dominated by spoil heaps and mining flashes, but outside your own back door you can make your very own little Garden of Eden. You often find it in mining communities, this love of green, growing things, a reaction perhaps to the dark, sterile world where the men spend their working lives. Mind you, none of them could compare with the house we came upon just outside the town, surrounded by a miniature golf course, complete with miniature flags and all. And around the house was a colony of plastic gnomes, always fishing, never catching, complete with a plastic menagerie of the more

Disney-ish denizens of the natural world. It was a suburban Utopia on the grand scale, yet here it was set in the middle of a mining area, a sort of Noddy-in-Pitland.

Once we were past Noddyland, we were back with the old-style pit village, and no messing. Alvecote is just about as basic as they come, and the National Coal Board even put notices on the houses in case anyone should be in doubt about the ownership. There's not a lot here, outside the one draughty main street, apart from an ancient priory, so ruinous that if you didn't know what it was, you'd pass it by without a second glance. Polesworth, next stop down the line, could boast something more tangible in the way of antiquities in Poole Hall, a gloomridden Tudor manor, stuck up high above the cut. I have never really been able to take to those dark Tudor houses, which may be interesting enough to visit but in which I should hate to live. So when we had moored for the night I turned my back on the solemnities of history and made for the flippancy of the pub. But there, it seemed, we had come at the wrong time. It was the final of the Ladies' Darts Competition. The place was packed with supporters cheering on their favourites. Everyone was having a great time, but it was no place for a stranger. I felt about as inconspicuous as a ham sandwich at a Bar Mitzvah. So I slunk away again into the night.

The following day we reached the Atherstone flight, and started to meet up with other people out on the canal for pleasure. The first encounter was with a family who gave us cheery greeting, told us about their vast experience of canal travel and then proceeded to give a demonstration by letting all the paddle gear drop with an horrendous clang. They went on to complain about the slow progress of the boat in front of them. I wandered up to investigate and found a young man in an outboard-powered sailing dinghy making his way single-handed up the locks. I went up the locks with him, and discovered he had just worked down from Birmingham and that this single-handed marathon was actually his introduction to canal travel. He said he was enjoying it, but thought he might stick to sailing in future. If I'd started off like that I'm not sure I'd have come back for more either. He did have the consolation of a nice, long, lock-free stretch up ahead – though not, to be sure, quite the loveliest stretch of waterway in England.

The canal now starts in on an astonishing succession of colour changes. As you get near to Hartshill, you can see a red shale poking out of the banks, and the water matches it, turning brick red. The whole area seems diseased – the red water mirrors a surface pockmarked with the excrescences of spoil. It takes a long time for a region to recover from such ravages, though some of the heaps do show a covering of scrubby grass and dwarfish trees. Then Hartshill Yard comes along, as welcome as an oasis in this grim desert. The first thing you see is a neat, busy, workmanlike sort of place, an elegantly ornate clock tower the only obvious embellishment. But look a bit closer and you have that special satisfaction of seeing ingenuity combined with grace. The covered dock, for example, comes off the canal at quite a sharp angle and, to avoid damage to the brickwork, the wall has been built on the curve so that boats will simply glance off if they hit. And how very pleasing that contrast between straight wall and curved wall can be.

After that you reach Nuneaton. At the canal end of the town you find yourself perched rather alarmingly above the steep cliff face of a huge quarry, and there's not much else of any interest in Nuneaton. It stands on a flat site, and the town seems to match its site, flat and dull. Housing is uniformly drab and insipid, and as you run past the backs you long for the terraces to part to give you a change of view. When they do open up, all they offer is a wide vista of even duller houses, and then you long for the houses to shut the view out again. At least there were allotments on the opposite bank, with garden sheds that showed far more ingenuity and sense of design than the houses. I stopped briefly to make a phone call. The phone didn't work. I went across to the shops. The shops were shut. That just about summed up Nuneaton for me.

When I got back to the boat, I noticed a doll's leg floating in the water, and it occurred to me that that made about the sixth I'd seen on the trip – never an arm, not a glimpse of a torso, not a head in sight, just legs, single legs, floating along all by themselves. That sort of thing can prey on your mind. Is there some strange doll's leg fetishist loose on the waterways? If there is I hope he stops in Nuneaton. They need something to liven the place up.

Beyond the town the water changes again to a grey-green slurry as you pass the quarries and the works that throw out a fine dust. It is a surreal landscape, ripped apart like a carcase. But work has started. An attempt is being made to put something back into the land from which so much has been taken. And in the process a new landscape is emerging. The high, conical hills are being grassed, but their very symmetry will signal to a later generation that there is nothing natural about the new hills.

At Hawkesbury Junction, the Coventry and the Oxford Canal meet. This is the home of the narrow boat *Friendship* and Rose Skinner. The Skinners were just about the last of the old breed of working boat

The cotton mill at Fazeley Junction.

people, 'Number Ones', living and working on their own boats. Now Joe is dead, and Rose spends her days standing in the cabin entrance, watching the world of the waterways go by. She has a cottage, but spends little time there. *Friendship* is home. As she says, she can never get used to going up and down stairs. She seems to take a pleasure in talking about the old days. She brought out a faded photograph of a youthful Joe, with his two mules, Dick and Ollie. He always said mules were better than horses for boat work. We talked for a while and then we were off, leaving Rose still standing in the cabin door. How many of us will be able to end our working days and look back at them with such real affection? It was a thought to keep in mind as we set off on the last five miles to Coventry, the centre of the car industry.

Just before I left on this trip, I was chatting to a friend who had recently been down the canal to Coventry. Very dull, he said. Well, there you are – one man's meat, and all the rest of it. I found it to be absolutely crammed with interest, loved every minute of it. The centre of Coventry has been rebuilt, but the old canal route takes you through two centuries of history, the centuries that saw Coventry emerge as a major industrial centre. Having been told how dull it was going to be, the first place of real significance caught me so entirely unawares that I just gaped in stupid amazement and practically ran the boat straight up the bank. As I disentangled myself from the branches of the willow I had steered us into, I thrust the tiller into someone else's hand, jumped ashore and ran back to see if I had really seen what I thought I had seen. There they were, all right, a little row of cottages, eighteenth-century, and obviously connected with domestic industry. They were not a bit like the weavers' cottages of Nantwich, for here the big workshop windows were on the ground floor. I knew exactly where I'd seen such windows before – in the Nottingham area where people used to knit hosiery on the stocking frames. For me, finding an old handworker's house like this is the next best thing to meeting an old hand worker himself. Let me explain.

The ground-floor windows really are big. In one cottage there is a huge multi-paned square, in the others the windows are like exaggerated cinemascope screens, very long but not very high. Now these are not very big cottages, and you have to think of all that well lit space occupied by the machines and the busy workers. Upstairs the tiny windows are cramped up under the eaves, filtering a dim light through to the living quarters of the house. The differences in style tell you that these were houses owned by independent workers, while the relative sizes of living and working areas tell you a good deal about the

price that had to be paid for that independence. You need time really to get behind the history of these cottages in the old village of Longford, but even a few minutes had told me quite a lot. One day I shall have to go back, and while I'm there I think I'll take a closer look at a story they tell about old Longford. Did the Baptists really immerse their adult converts in the Coventry Canal? I only hope it was a bit cleaner then than it is now, or that little ceremony must have sped a few of the faithful on their way to eternal bliss.

From old industry you move rapidly on to new industry, which makes quite a change for canal travellers who tend to see the scruffier end of the scruffier industries. You could easily end a long trip with the conviction that industrial development in Britain ended some where around the year 1900. Here you get places like Alfred Herbert, one of the world's most respected machine-tool makers, the factory surrounded by flower beds that would be a credit to the proudest gardener in Acacia Avenue. And there's Courtauld, the modern inheritors of the tradition that began with the domestic workers of centuries ago. They have new, elephantine grey buildings and what used to be called a smoke stack in the old days when coal fuelled industry, but is now just a fume stack. Whatever you call it, it's mighty big and impressive, reaching three hundred and sixty feet into the air. Not so far away is the slightly smaller but more ornate Victorian

Hawkesbury Junction, where the Oxford and Coventry Canals meet.

chimney of Cash's, and with Cash's you are right back with a chunk of industrial history.

Joseph Cash was one of those quirky individuals who seem to crop up among the ranks of Victorian industrialists. All around him he could see that the old ways of the textile workers were ending. Men no longer got up in the morning, climbed a few stairs and were ready to work at the loom. The power loom was writing finis to this way of life, even though the new ways were bitterly resented by the workers. Cash decided, through some bizarre reasoning, that what the old workers objected to was having to get out of the house to go to work, rather than the loss of independence and the need to work to a rigid time-table. So, Mr Cash built a block of houses around a central courtyard, and over these he placed his factory, the top shop. Down in the yard the steam engine worked, turning the looms, and at the start of each day the shrill of a whistle would send the men upstairs to work, popping up through trap doors in the floor like so many pantomime demons. At a second signal work began. There is no evidence that the weavers were any happier. But Cash's forms an odd little halfway stage between cottage and factory. And they still weave there. Even if the top shops are now only used for storage, looms clatter on in the courtyard factory, busily turning out name tags.

As textiles declined, the car industry grew and, lo and behold, right there by the canal is a sort of architectural metaphor for the whole process. The Coventry Cotton Factory was rebuilt after a fire in 1891, but by then no one was overanxious to start up the business again. It stood empty for five years, until Mr Henry Lawson came along and started two new businesses on the site. One was The Great Horseless Carriage Company. With a name like that it deserved to succeed, but it failed. The other company was Daimler. There's not much of the old factory left but, lurking in among the new, you can still catch a glimpse of one of the original Victorian buildings. By the time you've taken in that lot, you've reached the last bridge on the canal and you're through to Coventry Basin and the centre of the city. If you're interested in industrial history, then you'll find few more fascinating routes; if not, well it's still as pleasant a way as any to get to the city.

Coventry Basin is like Sheffield Basin in at least one respect: it is in the heart of the city, right on the edge of the busy inner ring road. But the character of the place is very different. Where Sheffield was enclosed and secretive, Coventry is very open, with a wide view across to the city spires. Down one side are old warehouses, with big wooden awnings, and the canal itself divides to run either side of a cobbled

Rose Skinner at Hawkesbury: she and her husband Joe were the last of the Number Ones, running a single horse-drawn narrow boat. Since Rose's death, the boat has gone to the waterways museum at Ellesmere Port.

peninsula. At the very end of the wharf is a little toll house, from which emerged a one-man welcoming committee from the Coventry Canal Society. He showed us round, took us to look at the exhibits they are starting to collect as a basis for a canal museum, and beat the drum in favour of the development of Coventry Basin. He need not have bothered: it should be obvious to anyone that, like Sheffield Basin, the place is just screaming for a proper use to be made of it. Here is an expanse of water, and usable water at that, flanked by buildings of character laden with historical associations. It is just too good to waste, and a city like Coventry, which lost so much of its past in war-time devastation, needs such places more than most.

In the post-war years Coventry became Britain's phoenix, the city that rose from the ashes of destruction. Reconstruction began in the days when we foolishly believed that the destruction of our cities had ended with the end of the war, not realizing that there was to be a period of whole scale demolition of our towns and cities more violent in its effect than anything Hitler managed to achieve. But Coventry is where the whole redevelopment business began, which makes it especially important. Coventry was the trendsetter, the father to all those shopping precincts you now find in almost every large town and city in the land. Coventry made its mistakes, but it had its successes too. For a start, the overall plan did try and take in the city centre as a whole, a complete unit. The traffic-free shopping area was a good, original idea and it was enlivened with things that were not strictly utilitarian: a tall aviary is great fun; sculpture in city streets a good idea. And they didn't stop at the shops. There was the Leofric Hotel, carefully integrated into the whole scheme and the Belgrade, a first-class new theatre. It was a bold scheme, put together with imagination. Boldest of all was the plan to build a new cathedral, something builders had not had a great deal of practice in over the past few hundred years. The reconstruction of Coventry was undertaken with spirit, with a determination to build well, to try and make up for what had been lost in those fearful raids.

The builders of the new Coventry were pioneers and, like all pioneers, they made mistakes which can easily be seen – with hindsight. The upper levels of the shopping precinct never really paid, simply because people were not encouraged to make the effort to trudge up there. The hopes for wide, open piazzas where people would sit around under big umbrellas sipping their drinks like seasoned *boulevardiers* were doomed by the climate. (Yet still they sit, those same sketchy figures, in hundreds of architects' plans.) But the main failure was the inability of

the architects to design individual shops of a quality that matched up to the quality of the overall plan. For all that, it was a brave new idea, and the tragedy has been that so many later developments have missed out the good things – the balanced community, the careful plan – and simply picked up the bad, cramming dull shops round a draughty square, where the sweet wrappers and cigarette packets whirl in the wind. The small traders have been relegated to the back streets, while the multiples monopolize the centres. At least Coventry shows you what might have been, and there are precious few successors that are even half as good.

I wandered around Coventry in the evening. I wandered around for a long time, partly because I was looking for a decent pub, and it took a long time to dawn on me that the place just didn't have one, or if it did, I'd never find it. What Coventry at night does have, however, is a magnificent skyline, when the two great spires, the old cathedral's and St John's, are picked out by floodlights. Seen by day, the former is a ruin, dignified even in destruction, but a ruin none the less; and both churches are thickly coated with industrial grime. But in the lights, all that is lost, and each detail stands out with a clarity that would surely have delighted the medieval masons. The top of the spire of St John's, reaching up towards the night sky, seemed far more remote than did the pale disc of the moon, hovering just behind it. Then I walked to the new cathedral, Coventry's most famous building. Sadly, I have

Cash's top shops in Coventry; the workers lived in the lower part of the building and came up to the top floor to work.

never been able to love it. I remember coming here shortly after it was completed and thinking that at first sight it was not unlike an overgrown Odeon, and now that old judgement came straight back to mind. There are things I like, especially the statue of St Michael, but that little stumpy spire is the first thing that draws the eye. I know the architect wanted to avoid the clash with the tall spire of the old cathedral, but wouldn't it have been better to have omitted the spire altogether? The inside is a very different matter, with the rich colours of the tall lancet windows in the nave spilling their bright patterns out over the floor. And at night that interior is a marvel, a world of mysterious shadows, so that when the eye moves up the cathedral seems, like the old spires, to reach out towards an infinity of darkness.

As I walked away from the new cathedral, I must confess my thoughts shifted back to less ethereal matters, and I returned to pub hunting. I finished up in a place in Corporation Street, and was frisked on the way in. A very polite gentleman patted my pockets and came on the boat key, which was fastened to a plastic float, shaped rather like a small hand grenade. That really got him quite excited until the object was produced. Obviously, and very sadly, such precautions are essential in some parts, but they do not contribute to relaxation and jollity. Not that there was very much of either in the place. Perhaps I was reading things into the atmosphere, but there seemed to be an air of desperation about the way in which people stood around with fixed grins, as though they were trying to convince themselves they were having a great time. Coventry was going through a bad patch just then, so maybe people just kept on laughing, hoping the bad news would go away. Or maybe it is all part of the general big-city malaise, the death of the city centre, the retreat to suburbia. Maybe I simply had indigestion. Whatever the reason, I sank my pint and got back to the boat. Then, back at the basin, I turned and took a last look at those magical spires.

CHAPTER 13

Homage to Brindley

We eventually got back to Hawkesbury and to the journey south, as we left the Coventry Canal for the Oxford. It is here that the canal again returns to the country, performing its now familiar conjuring trick of transforming itself from a man-made transport route into a comfortable part of the natural world.

All around the countryside heaved itself into a steady roll, like a gentle sea swell. Copses and coverts dotted the hills, tall trees stood proud above hedgerows. The oppressive cloud that had dogged our travels broke, and the seasons at last seemed to have accepted their obligation to follow a proper course. Spring had arrived, and the animals were turned on as if someone had thrown a switch. Two stallions reared at each other, waving their hooves like sparring boxers, while the young mare, the object of all this male bravado, chewed placidly away at the fresh grass. The stallions gave up in disgust, and raced each other around the field for a change. Turning the corner, another field and a cow that had given birth only moments before. The calf, propped up precariously on shaking, splayed-out legs, was being licked clean, made decent to join the rest of life. Somewhere in the distance a chiff-chaff sang the absurd, repetitive song that gives it its name. Rabbits sat up to peer at us, were none too impressed with what they saw, and presented us with a view of rapidly retreating, bobbing, white scuts.

We feel comfortable; yet this is, in fact, a very artificial line. Once the Oxford Canal wandered all over the countryside, but as part of the nineteenth-century improvement, a new straight line was dug, and the old line comes and goes as a series of reedy loops. I have followed a few of the old lines. Often they seem to vanish altogether, and then you suddenly find a hump-backed canal bridge set down in the middle of a field, looking sadly forlorn. But even this aggressively straight route has been absorbed into the country as shrubs flower on the banks and the hard edges soften with use. We soon came upon two later intrusions – the main railway fine heading south for London, offering a somewhat quicker route than the canal could provide, and the M6 motorway. The newer the route, the more intrusive it inevitably seems to be; yet, given time, the new and the old become just the old and the older, and in the process they seem somehow to come closer together. At Ansty there was a short row of tile-roofed cottages with, in the middle, a single building with a thatched roof. Once they would all have been thatch, and now there was just this solitary survivor. Yet time has brought them together, for the tiled roofs have sagged and swayed so that their lines, too, have the swinging curves of thatch. Unity is restored; and unity and harmony seemed the themes of the day, as we slipped between woods and fields and the sun shone on us until we left it for the temporary dark of Newbold tunnel and a mooring for the night at the far end.

Newbold offers a number of delights. For those who enjoy exploration there is one of those lengths of abandoned canal which includes an old tunnel. You can see the entrance down by the church. Later in the evening we sampled another of those delights: the Boat Inn. It is an example of one way the British pub could develop; we had recently

The Oxford Canal at Fenny Compton: originally this was a tunnel but was later opened up to create the deep cutting.

stopped at the Greyhound at Hawkesbury Junction which offered another way. The Greyhound has long been famed as a historical canal pub. Many's the thousands of boatmen and women who have drunk there in the old days. Now the dead hand of the 'improver' has been laid on it. Carpet covers the old quarry tiles, the beer pumps have gone, and – well, you can fill in the rest. Gentility seems to be the new

keynote. It's a common enough story. The Boat is a place that has taken a different tack. In fact my only complaint is that they've got a damn silly sign, showing a great schooner beating through a force-nine gale. I've seen a few gales on my travels, but I've never seen a schooner on the Oxford Canal. The Boat offers you good beer and good society. The beer is traditional Davenport's, and a good part of the social life revolves around the skittles alley. Skittles is a great game which comes in a whole variety of forms. In our part of the world we have 'Aunt Sally', but this one was new to me. The skittles themselves were the familiar wooden pins, but instead of the usual ball the missile was a thick, round wooden disc, called a cheese, which you threw with a sort of backhand flip. The great virtue of this game was that there was really no limit to the number who can play it. Having wandered across to see the locals in action, we were simply absorbed into the competition. The rules are simplicity itself. You throw your cheese at the skittles, and the following player has to match or better your score. If he doesn't, he loses a 'life', and if you lose an agreed number of lives you are eliminated. So it goes on, until there's just one player left. It is a wonderfully sociable game, which allows strangers to join and enjoy the life of the locals' local. And that's surely what the pub should be – a sociable place. The beer's good, but in the end it's really there to loosen the tongue and ease the path of conversation. If I have an argument with CAMRA, the Campaign for Real Ale: it is that they make the beer seem all-important instead of seeing it as just part of the whole pub scene.

The following day we were to call back to Hillmorton for fuel, gas and that all-important pump out. It was Saturday, the busy day for the hire fleet, so we had agreed to get there by eight in the morning, which meant a seven o'clock start. Once you've actually made the effort to drag yourself out of bed, there is a special pleasure in travelling in the early morning, when the rest of the world is just beginning to stir. You find a tranquillity, a stillness of the water that it seems almost indecent to disturb. There was no real mist, just a series of grey wisps that sat, quite motionless, over the grey, mirroring water, a breath of vapour through which only the early insects moved. It was to be the last moment of tranquillity we would see that day. As we reached the yard and got on with the jobs, the other boats started piling in as holiday makers returned from their week's outing. Manoeuvring out of the tight little basin became just a mite tricky. Then we retraced the path we had taken four weeks before, this time following in the wake of *Lynx*, a working narrow boat with fifteen tons of coal on board. In front of us the painted stern was low in the water, while the steersman leaned with professional nonchalance, snug in that comfortable little space where the roof hatch slides away, and you can stand with the cabin doors closed behind you, keeping out the draught. Lovely to see a seventy-foot boat slip so easily in and out of constricted spaces, to the accompaniment of the deep gurgle of the prop and the steady throb of the engine. At Braunston our ways parted and we set off for Napton, water shortages, restrictions and all kinds of problems.

At Napton the new strict regulations came into force, with locks open for only three hours a day, from noon to three in the afternoon. In theory we should have had plenty of time, but ahead of us was *Malta* – a converted seventy-foot narrow boat being worked by a completely inexperienced steerer and the boat's owner, a woman with an injured wrist. The poor man at the tiller was doing his best, but the boat was being brought down to Oxford after a refit and repairs to the hull, and you could actually see the distraught owner wince at every bump and graze. And the more she winced, the more harassed the steersman became, until he was reduced to a state of near paralysis, stuck in the middle of the cut, calling out 'What do I do? What do I do?' My offer of help was not altogether altruistic. If we wanted to get up the flight that day, then *Malta* had to be got up first. Leaving them to get the boat in and out of the locks, I looked after the paddles. It was hot work dashing around the locks like a winding dervish and there was less time than I should have liked for looking around. But I snatched a moment to take in that pleasant stagger of locks bending up around the hill that is topped by Napton windmill, with its curved silvery cap like the dome of a Russian church. It seemed to be all work but, with a lot of sweating and heaving, we got the old lady up. 'What's that?' said the lock keeper, peering down as the bows came round the last bend. 'That's never *Malta*, is it?' He shook his head at the thought of times past. 'Fastest boat on the Union she were.'

Having got *Malta* up and on her way, I had to wait for our own, less romantic boat to come and join us. And, while I waited, three o'clock struck. To my horror the lock keeper prepared to slam the padlock closed on the lock gates. I argued and pleaded and eventually had to dash off and find a phone box to get authority from the foreman to pass through that last lock which would give us the entry to eleven lock-free miles above. We got permission, and went on our way along one of the most remarkable stretches of canal in the country.

James Brindley was the chief engineer who laid down the line of the Oxford Canal, and you don't need to read a book to find that out.

The information is written down for you in the amazing convolutions of the canal itself. Brindley was a great believer in 'contour cutting', following the same level for as long as possible, and he also favoured a long summit to act as a reservoir. So, having got his canal up the hill at Napton, he was in no great hurry to get it down again. He must have come up here on his old mare and eyed this rolling country with some dismay before setting off to thread his way round the humps and hollows, like a man hunting for the exit to a maze. He made it all right, and he created a route of the most bewildering twists and turns. You come under a bridge, look away to your right, and there you see what appears to be another canal and another bridge on a course parallel with your own. But it's not: it's either where you're going, or where you've just been, impossible to tell which. Landmarks as solid and immovable as a tall radio mast seem to skip quite wantonly around the land, appearing in front, behind or at either side. At Wormleighton one reaches the ultimate in bends as the canal almost forms a circle round the hill, a moat to Wormleighton House. It does, at least, provide the opportunity to view a very fine house from all sides. I envy the occupants their view, and I am even more envious of the splendid wrought-iron veranda which graces their home. Some say that this exaggerated loop was made simply as part of the contour cutting plan, but I believe it has more to do with our old friends the gentry, in this case Earl Spencer. The Oxford Canal Committee minute book records the information that by not building locks 'the navigators will have no business to stop, so that the apprehended danger will be the less on that account.' In other words,

The former maintenance yard at Claydon.

if the boatmen can't stop, they can't pinch his lordship's pheasants, nor his maids' bottoms.

On either side of the canal, the hills rise in slow, gentle curves that seem to arrange themselves into a succession of perfectly balanced pictures. A line of trees climbs the skyline, then stops just short of the hill top, so that the shape of the hill itself is suddenly clear, and the bare top becomes the focal point of the whole scene. The line of trees bordering the towpath suddenly breaks and you see right over the greenery of the wide valley towards a whitewashed pub some two miles away, which I recognized as the place we planned to moor for the night. And no sooner had we got used to that view than the canal took another of its wild swings and we found ourselves retreating from our destination at good speed. Dear Mr Brindley, your canal may not be the most practical transport route in the world, your twists and turns may have been the despair of those who had to earn a living on the water, but those of us who come this way for pleasure can only offer you our very sincere thanks.

Our idyll was broken by the busy traffic erupting from the marina at Fenny Compton. It makes for an appalling, quite inexcusable smugness to see so many people making such a hash of things, but then the great majority were probably taking out boats for the first time and coping as best they could. And when I think back to my own first efforts – well, that is a great corrective to smugness. But I remember getting very careful instruction before I set out, and I do wonder if all hire firms take their responsibilities seriously enough and tell their customers about the rules of the waterways. People who seem to act in a wholly antisocial manner often do so from pure ignorance. Some need more instruction than others. I'd just come round a corner and poked the boat's nose into a narrow bridge hole when I saw a second boat, several yards away, pointing straight at me. I couldn't hear what was being said by the woman at the tiller, and I didn't need to. The look of utter horror on her face said it all. Her mouth open in a soundless scream, she pushed the tiller hard over and, with engine still going full bore, drove her boat straight up the bank. If the bank had been just a bit lower, I reckon she'd have been halfway down the cornfield before she came to a stop; as it was, I don't suppose there was a bit of crockery left unbroken on that whole boat.

We eventually arrived at Fenny Compton, but it was late in the evening before the unhappy steerer of *Malta* appeared, minus the boat. They had broken down and he was looking sadly, and with little success, for a mechanic. In the end, all he could do was trudge the long

The old blacksmith's forge at Claydon maintenance yard: the buildings have subsequently been restored

miles back to see if self-help could do where professional help was not to be had. And they made it. As we set off in a leisurely way at ten in the morning, *Malta* came limping in. Poor souls: they had been on the go since half past five. That was the last we were to see of them on the trip, but when I got back home I was delighted to see the old boat safe in its Oxford moorings.

Having survived Napton, we were confronted by the next batch of restrictions. Claydon locks were only three miles away, but they were not going to be open until midday, so we made a very staid and steady progress, telling each other how nice it was not to hurry. Hurry? The rate we were moving, we could have been overtaken by an energetic snail.

In sharp contrast to the previous day, our route that morning lay down a dead straight cutting. This was not the result of a change of heart by James Brindley, for once upon a time this had been a tunnel through the low hill. But it had proved a troublesome affair and in the nineteenth century they simply took its top off. Today, although you have nothing but the sky overhead, it is still known as Fenny Compton Tunnel. At the far end, we stopped, nipped up the bank to peer into Wormleighton reservoir and then hopped back down again pretty smartly. One look at it, half dried up, and you certainly knew why the water restrictions were needed.

At Claydon, we joined the back of the queue and waited. This is a place I fell in love with years ago and for a brief, glorious moment it seemed that we would actually be able to take over the old canalside buildings and convert them into a home. But the difficulties were too great, the cost too high and the splendid dream vanished. Someone else has been luckier, or more persevering, and the buildings are being restored. It is a marvellous site, isolated among the fields, a little L-shaped group of buildings next to the lock. One branch of the 'L', at right angles to the lock, is the old smithy with its central forge. Even the old leather bellows have been left in place. Standing there, I could still see it as the heart of the home we had planned. I envy those who are moving in and wish them well – but how the envy doth over-ride the good wishes. If I'd stayed there much longer, I'd have become a maudlin wreck, weeping for what might have been. If I had been the new owner I might have been weeping anyway. There used to be a pleasant block of stables on the other side of the canal and some insensitive soul has crudely bricked them all up.

At twelve, the convoy got under way. We all moved off down the locks in a series of fits and starts until we got near Cropredy, where the whole procession reformed as the canal was reduced to a muddy wallow. Everyone seemed to have different views of how to cope with a canal narrowed to half its width and reduced to half its normal depth. Some opted for the brute force approach, furiously revving the engine, trying to push a way through like a battering ram. The only result of that was that they drove their sterns deeper down into the mud, which was thrown up as a thick, brown churning mess behind them. Others kept their engine just ticking over, and found things went quite well so long as they could stick squarely in the middle of the channel.

The real nuisance about these stoppages is that they just don't give you a chance to stand and stare. You have to be at so-and-so at three, and if you are late you are liable to spend the best part of a day kicking your heels in the middle of nowhere. Cropredy, you see, is just the sort of place any right-minded person would want to stop. It is an old settlement set at one of the crossing points of the River Cherwell, a fact which gave Cropredy its one moment of unwelcome fame when it was the site of a Civil War battle in 1644. Today it is one of those villages in which Oxfordshire is so blissfully rich, a close-set place of rich, ironstone buildings. It is a lovely stone, full of tones of grey, yellow and reddish-brown, that seems not so much to reflect the light as to absorb it, taking the warm glow deep into its very heart.

Somerton deep lock on the Oxford Canal: it is clear how it got its name.

In the afternoon we made our way to Banbury. It is old but on a main road, and the traffic has almost overwhelmed the place. The famous lady on the white horse would find it an uncomfortable experience riding to Banbury Cross these days. It is a market town, serving a rural area, and it's industrial. They used to make plush velvet in these parts. Inevitably, the first glimpse you get from the canal is of the industrial area. You come into the town past the new industrial estate that provides most of the local employment. There is an extraordinary uniformity in the buildings – they are all dull. Then you meet the lock in the middle of the town. Once this was the site of the town wharf, surrounded by old, red-brick warehouses. Various schemes were put forward for using the old buildings, and then the council had a better idea. Today it is a draughty bus station, and all but one of the buildings has gone. The sole survivor has been converted into a youth club, and very well converted too. The original idea had been to use all the old buildings as the basis for a leisure centre, and the one success does show that it would have been very possible. Now there is a new leisure centre, Spiceball Park, which sounds like a cross between a Chinese restaurant and one of P. G. Wodehouse's country estates. Conversion would surely have been cheaper, but I suspect it was a wish to be up to date, modern. It reminds me of a village shop I visited in Ireland. When you bought anything, the woman at the counter would take your money, write out a bill, screw it all up into a metal cylinder and with a twitch of the wires send it whirring off to the cashier. Some time in the past, no one could quite remember when, they had been convinced that was the modern way to run a business. So it might be, but not in a shop where the cashier sits a full two yards from the assistant.

The mill conversion is a mark of the new attitude that is steadily gaining in force, the one that says 'do not wantonly destroy what is good in order to replace it with what is worse'. I hope, though, that when councils, or anyone else, do take over old buildings and convert them, they take a good look at any legal obligations they might be inheriting. We spent the evening in Banbury with a group from Leamington, one of whom had been at Birmingham Art College, and he told the following salutary tale. He was a regular visitor to the club rooms that occupied the old stables at Gas Street. Showing the curiosity proper to a student, he unearthed the interesting information that the occupants of the stable were obliged to provide fodder for any bona fide canal boat horse. Well, the next step was obvious. He borrowed Caggy Stevens's old horse Mac and duly presented him at the bar. The club did their best and I'm told Mac had a very pleasant evening supping draught bitter. So, gentlemen, look to your leases.

The next day we had managed to get ourselves a start from the right side of the closed lock, so we could look forward to clearing the irksome

restrictions altogether before the end of the day. We were faced with the delightful prospect of again being able to take our own time, relax and enjoy a day of superb scenery. There are no spectacular eruptions of nature, no tall crags, no deep gorges, but if someone who did not know Britain came to me and said, 'I've heard all about England's green and pleasant land. Show me something of old rural England', I might very well ask him to join me for a day on the southern Oxford. It is a landscape as English as village cricket.

The route the canal takes is the route of the river Cherwell, which starts as little more than a stream making its way as best it can, wriggling through the land. Then, as it gathers strength, it gradually straightens and its banks, lined with stands of spiky willows like a procession of angry porcupines, rise higher above the water. The river dictates much that happens along the way. Settlements were sited at fords; mills lined the banks, taking their power from the stream; the lush meadowland spread out into the valley. Since then the importance of the river has declined, but the settlements and many of the mills still stand, even if the wheels no longer turn.

Travel that day was marked by a pleasant stagger of locks, not enough to make for hard work, but enough to give the day an easy, stop-start rhythm. You could add to that the Oxford Canal specialities, the charming little lift bridges, very simple things, no more than a wooden platform and a pair of sturdy balance beams stuck out at an angle so that you can move them. It was a quiet day of overall contentment with a few special places that linger in the mind.

The unusual diamond shaped lock on the Oxford Canal connects the latter to the River Cherwell.

There was Twyford Mill, grandest of all the Cherwell mills, which illustrated a strange phenomenon: the tall buildings were typical of the early mills, but the new could hardly be described as buildings at all. They stretched. The more you put in, the larger the flexible buildings became, so they sat in their various states of fullness like marquees in different stages of erection. Beyond that was the tall spire of King's Sutton church, a bold outline on the horizon. Then at Nell Bridge we came to one of the few places where the twentieth century makes a firm mark on the land. The A41 crosses the canal on a flat concrete bridge, yet the old canal world still manages to hang on. The original arch has been kept under the new, so that to pass under this most modern of bridges, you have to thread your boat through the oldest and narrowest of bridge holes. So on we went to Somerton deep. We were too early in the year to see it at its best. For that you must come here in summer, when you will find the little tail bridge in bloom, wild flowers thrusting out from every crack in the brickwork. Perhaps it always seems so perfect because you know what is lurking just around the corner – Upper Heyford.

I was down this way four years ago, when we came round a bend to find a seventy-foot narrow boat rammed solid under a bridge arch. The steerer had missed the centre and it was now almost immoveable. We heaved and strained, and all the while the planes came in. FIIIs screaming low overhead, so low you automatically ducked every time one came past. The noise was shattering, for we were stuck right at the end of the main runway of the USAF base. Poor Upper Heyford, a delightful little village, with one of the biggest and busiest airfields in the country right on its doorstep. The old thatched cottage looks out on the tenpin bowling rink; the village band competes with the patriotic airs sung by the ladies' choir from the base. Down at the base they have created little America, much as the colonials used to create little Englands in their old imperialist days.

Upper Heyford has to have a Lower Heyford. Here is a village that has grown within the framework of its own past, where change has come slowly. It is a meeting place, where the canal is crossed by the old Chipping Norton-Bicester road, just the spot you would expect to find developing as a small trading centre. Expectations are not disappointed. Everything seems to cluster around the centre, with the railway station opposite the wharf. Road buildings, canal buildings, railway buildings, warehouses, stables, station – pick them all up, shuffle them and deal them out in a new order and nothing would really seem out of place. The local ironstone unifies them all.

The village of Lower Heyford, with its squat comfortable church, presiding like a father over a tight clutter of little houses, did see one moment of violent change. When Brindley came here he decided to dig a new channel for the river, to make room for his canal. Heyford Mill looks a splendid old building, but it only dates back to 1788, for an older mill stood on the east bank of the old river, and the present mill stands on the west bank of the new. It must have seemed that the world was being turned topsy-turvy, but the changes register now to no one but the historian. The eye receives no surprises. Outside Heyford, man has again rearranged Nature to produce, in Rousham Park, one of the earliest and loveliest of the great landscape gardens of England. It is an ordering that has nothing to do with the formalities of a Versailles, and everything to do with the British love of compromise. Nature is tamed, made to jump through the gardener's hoops; but you still get the feeling that if ever the cage door was opened, Nature would be wild and free again.

Places tick by, the Rock of Gibraltar – another Gibraltar, another stone quarry – and beyond that river and canal mingle, so that the bends and twists of Brindley's canal become, for just a short while, the natural twists of the Cherwell. I am very close to my own back door. Shipton on Cherwell, the church by the canal, then Thrupp comes up around the corner with its pub and little row of cottages facing the water, the lift bridge and the mill cottages. The mill itself was bought up by the canal company, but they only wanted the water and the building has long gone. Over the fields is Hampton Gay, a tiny church where you can see the graves of the poor unfortunates who travelled on the train which toppled over the bridge into the frozen water of the canal on Christmas Eve 1874. Hampton Gay itself is as dead as those passengers. DMVs the archaeologists call such places – deserted medieval villages – humps in the ground to the rest of us, where the kids used to dig around for the odd pot sherd. Were they medieval, or modern Woolworths? If you're young enough it doesn't make very much difference. Beyond that is the burnt-out shell of the old manor house, a mixture of decay and unlikely preservation. Rooks' nests fill the chimney, trees grow through the wall, yet a window catch remains intact, as though someone could come back one day and close the window. At the back of the manor is the ice house, a hole in the ground surrounded by thick stone walls, an Elizabethan deep-freeze. There's a lot to see in this little corner – the ruins of the old paper mill, for instance – but I had other preoccupations. As soon as the boat was moored I was off to the nearest call-box. In just a short while the family appeared and I sneaked off for a a night at home. Next morning, though, it was back on board for Oxford and the Thames.

CHAPTER 14

Down the Thames

The last few miles from Thrupp take you round the back end of Kidlington. Sometimes going round the back of a town means missing the best part of it, but not so with Kidlington, which is an almost perfect example of unplanned, uncontrolled, ribbon development. If you look in and around the place, especially the area near the church, you'll find old Kidlington, a good, solid Oxfordshire village, but you have to look hard to find it. For the rest, it streams out along the main Oxford-Banbury road, and if it was not for the railway and the canal which get in the way it might well have kept going to Banbury. This kind of development is inevitably formless. There can be no obvious focal point, which makes it all the harder for a place to stop becoming just a place and start becoming a community. But the canal traveller is spared all this. The canal passes along the backs of gardens, quite surprisingly long gardens they are, as well, the sort you get with many old cottages, gardens intended for use. We came across one very un-English practice. Two households had got together and knocked down the fence between the two properties to make one really big garden. I've seen this sort of thing in America, but never here. If the Englishman's home is his castle, then the garden is his moat.

Beyond Kidlington, you can take a short cut across to the Thames, but I wanted to stay with the canal into the centre of Oxford. The city is traditionally divided between town and gown. We got town: Morris Radiators, not Merton College; British Leyland rather than Christ Church. But the journey in is not all works, and you get a good, attractive bit of town. You start with the big houses, lawns down to the water, and just a touch of Oxford culture when you see sculpture in the garden, solid, chunky things in iron, art with a capital A. Then the industry comes in, and after that it's Jericho. This is very much the Oxford the tourist doesn't see, little streets of small, brick, terraced houses. This is more than an enclave in an opulent city, it is a community in its own right. They build in stone for the grand buildings in the centre, but down here it is just the humble brick in a distinctive local style. It is a district with a strong character all its own, as individual as the Italianate brick church of St Barnabas that lords it over the whole area.

Isis lock appears, crossed by an elegant iron foot-bridge, smart in new black and white paint. Beyond that is Upper Fisher Row where the boatman's chapel once floated – an odd little boat it was, complete with a wooden church tower, quite tiny, but big enough to take the congregation. This is the way the canal used to go before the old basin disappeared beneath car parks and Nuffield College. I can't think there was much of a gain, since Nuffield is the one college in Oxford with practically no architectural distinction whatsoever. But our route lay in another direction. At the bottom of the lock, we turned sharp right to join the river as it wandered off round the back of the station.

The canal gives you one view of Oxford, the river another, at first far less charming. For you are shunted round the back of the new Westgate development. Instead of the hoped-for colleges, you get acres of car park. Oxford and the motor car are engaged in perpetual warfare, but whether the battle can be won by laying waste great tracts such as this seems, to put it mildly, doubtful. It is a shame that neither canal nor river takes you into the other Oxford, for it is a place with much to offer. In the years since I moved to the area my affection for the place has grown. It is not just that it is full of such architectural splendours as the Radcliffe Camera, the Sheldonian, the college buildings, the marvellous facade of Broad Street, but it can also be a very human, intimate city. The Bodleian Library is one of the world's greatest and can boast in Duke Humphrey's Library something as close to the ideal of an ancient, scholarly seat of learning as you'll ever see. Yet you don't have to use the Bod for very long before the staff greet you by name.

Things start to improve when you reach Folly Bridge with its strange little flint building, full of niches from which the stone heads have gazed out over generations of undergraduates wrestling with the art of punting. I doubt if there is an activity in the world at which it is easier to look a complete idiot than punting. One glorious June day I went out with a friend keen to renew his acquaintance with the craft, and he soon showed that he had lost none of his old skill. We were resting on the grassy bank of the Cherwell up above Magdalen Bridge when another punt came down propelled with great panache by a young man who was obviously making a tremendous impression on his female companion. Up came the pole, clean and vertical – just at the moment alas, that the punt was shooting under a low foot-bridge. The punt shot on. The pole and punter did not. I continue to leave punting to friends.

There was no one punting that day. It was cold, with a threat of rain in the wind, as we pulled out by Christ Church meadows and the Isis became the Thames proper. This is very much rowing territory. Boat houses and College barges line the banks. Fine things those barges, ornate almost to the point of vulgarity; sad to think that their best days are gone. But, at least, as you look back now across the meadows, you do get to see that other Oxford, the University city. Ah, people say, there are the dreaming spires, but I have never understood what Arnold meant by that phrase.

Travelling by river is not in the least like travelling by canal. You get few back doors here but quite a few front doors, opulent front doors, not to say conspicuously opulent. And you get the word 'No' – No Fishing, No Landing, No Bathing, No Mooring. It seems to crop up all the time, everywhere you look, on large, ugly notice boards threatening untold horrors to anyone who so much as hitches a rope to a post embedded in the sacred, private land. And it's been going on for at least a century. Even Jerome K. Jerome, in that best of all books about the Thames, *Three Men in a Boat*, complained of the practice, and the erectors of notice boards were threatened not only with a violent demise but with the even more appalling fate of having Harris sing comic songs on their graves. I know just how he felt. It is not so much the desire of the riverside owner for privacy that offends; it is the accumulation of so many 'Noes', one after the other, that gets you down. You start to feel shifty, an unwelcome intruder in a closed world. Eric de Maré, the author of my other favourite Thames book, *Time on the Thames*, put forward a proposal for turning the river into a sort of linear National Park, but nothing ever came of it. A pity, for this can be a marvellous river. I first travelled the river from Oxford to London in an old-fashioned wooden canoe for one splendid summer week some eighteen years ago. Perhaps it was all too perfect then, for the new reality was not living up to the old memory. Those discouraging prohibitions marked the start of a slow, sad disillusionment with the Thames.

A fine drizzle set in, which did little to improve the mood. The river craft did not help much either. A new breed of craft has appeared in recent years and they are quite depressingly ugly. Of course, new boats are seldom welcome. Jerome used to complain about the steam launches of his day, but when I met one on the way it seemed quite superb, slim and sleek, all gleaming mahogany and shiny brass. But these new creations are wide, flat, blunt things, made out of fibre-glass, looking for all the world like floating bath tubs. So in a spirit of damp gloom, we puttered on towards Abingdon where, of a sudden, the gloom lifted. The weather was no better, but I know no town that

This lock at Abingdon is typical of Thames locks, with the lock cut to one side of the river and the broad weir on the other.

presents a more varied and interesting face to the river. Jerome thought it dull, but, for once, I am in total disagreement.

The streets of Abingdon run down to the water, little streets that look as though they ought to be heading somewhere but just vanish in wet, cobbled slopes. Abingdon is no place for drunken, midnight rambles. There was an abbey here once, but that is long gone, leaving the fifteenth-century abbey gateway as an entrance to nowhere. But just look around at what does remain, and you find an object lesson in the ways in which the old can be taken, adapted and revitalized. Look at Abingdon's gaol, a solid octagonal block that was put up in the rush of gaol building at the end of the eighteenth century. Seen from the outside little has changed. It has been cleaned up, and in the cleaning the essential characteristics have been highlighted: the random rubble walls, chunky stones set together in a higgledy-piggledy manner which somehow manages to emphasize their strength and durability; the small windows, black grilles contrasting with the pale stone. Inside is a whole complex of functions – art gallery, theatre, gymnasium, swimming pool. And the same robust style characterizes even the small details, like the stencil lettering for signs, or the unfussy, plain, wooden panels that screen the public telephones. It all looks obvious now that it's finished, but it took an act of imagination to take the decrepit gaol and make it into something so splendid.

Abingdon is a town of very civilized virtues. It has a complex street pattern, and a complex house pattern that covers a whole range of styles and periods. There are individual buildings of quality, like the Market Hall with its little cupola. There is a museum at the top of the Hall from which you look down the streets that spread away from the Square and you can see how the town has grown. And if you go down again for a closer look you discover how individual buildings have adapted to the old street plan. Helen Street, curving away down to the church, displays a rich variety of houses: number 21, bow-fronted, dignified Georgian; number 23, next door, squeezed in and up to the little dormers in the attic; 27A, a sort of afterthought to 27, built in the old Oxford vernacular of alternate grey and red bricks. Materials vary from brick to ashlar, colour washes give houses their own individual hues. Styles, roof lines, everything alters. Yet it reads as a whole, makes its own statement, satisfies. The twentieth century has added a shopping precinct.

We stopped the night at Clifton Hampden, on the recommendation of a lock keeper's wife, a splendid, chatty, helpful person. The Barley Mow at Clifton Hampden is another candidate for the oldest-pub-in-Britain stakes. It was certainly built in the days when people were a good deal shorter than they are today, as I once discovered by braining myself when I walked in. But we had no chance to pay a visit, for the old building suffered from a fire recently, and they were still putting the roof back. It might have been sad if there had not been a splendid substitute on the opposite bank.

Next day we headed down to Goring Gap, the great 'V' cut out by the river on its way through the Chilterns. Goring and Streatley are two villages, Goring on the Oxfordshire bank, Streatley on the Berkshire. The river divides between lock and weir and mill stream, crossed by a profusion of little bridges. My very elderly Thames guide describes the scene as 'the quintessence of the picturesque', and I cannot quarrel with that. We picked up a couple of hitchhikers at Goring, two ducks that came and sat on the cabin roof and stayed there, even when we moved off from the moorings, long enough to satisfy themselves they had scrounged all there was to be scrounged. Like Trafalgar Square pigeons, these ducks have become professional beggars.

Along the Thames, you can scarcely help noticing the opulence of riverside houses. There are lots of those stockbroker-Tudor places with lawns that look as though they've been trimmed with nail scissors; quite a few neo-Georgians, more neo than Georgian, and just a few neo-Gothic. The saving grace of the neo-Gothics is that they are actually fun. If you are going to be ostentatious, then you might just as well be riotously ostentatious, and down by the Thames a few have really let themselves go. There are turrets and parapets, cupolas and domes that seem to have been borrowed from the Kremlin, pinnacles and verandas and there are a few houses that look remarkably like the home invented by Charles Addams for his famous monstrous family.

The extravagance begins to fade as you get closer to Reading and the dreariest section of the whole river. You get a view of the old gaol where Oscar Wilde wrote his ballad, the Huntley and Palmer factory, a solidly respectable Victorian building that one would once have described as typical of the town, and the new blocks. And the gasometer. You can see it for miles, and I have often wondered what myopic planner ever gave permission for such a structure on such a site. Reading is Britain's average town. Whenever the market research lads want to try out Brand X, they trundle it over to Reading. If it gets the thumbs-up there, then it's straight into the shops; thumbs-down, and it's back to the drawing board. I sometimes get this awful thought: are we doomed to live in a land where everything ends up Reading-style? Looking around at the bland, drabness of the town, the awful, dull, flat anonymity, the prospect seems too hideous to contemplate.

Reading marked the place where we had to stop while I collected a license to navigate the Thames. Up to then, I had only had a scrap of paper which all the lock keepers cheerfully signed, confirming that I was passing their lock with no legal authority whatsoever. A curious system. I was told that all I had to do was pop into Reading and collect the official documents. I should have known better than to expect any encounter with official documents to be either swift or painless. To obtain a licence you have to complete forms, and to get the forms you have to queue behind others wanting the same forms. In this case, I was waiting behind two small boys trying to licence a dinghy. The Thames Conservancy insist that you have a name for your craft, however humble, and that name must be unique.

'How about Jaws?' asked one boy.

'We've had twenty-three already this year,' said the official, stonily.

'Seagull?'

This time she only snorted. And so it went on. Every name had been used.

'White Cloud?'

'It would be White Cloud V.'

On and on it went. In the end I joined in the game, but my notions fared no better than theirs. At last they decided to go away and think

The attractive river frontage at Abingdon, dominated by the tall spire of the church, with the 15th century almshouses alongside to the left.

and I was left with the form which wanted to know, among other things, the area of the boat in square metres. And when I'd finally worked out that, they informed me they didn't need the information anyway. At least the licence to cruise a hundred miles of Thames was cheaper than the one to travel a mile and a half of Rochdale Canal. I came out of the office to find a thin, hard rain being smacked into my face by a bitter, stinging wind. Work became a misery. When you come to a lock on the canal, you jump out and busy yourself. On the Thames it is all done for you, but you have to cut the engine and hold the boat into the side with the ropes. In the wet, those ropes become like things possessed. They coil themselves stiffly around you, trip you up, grasp at you. And when you get them in place, you just have to stand there listening to the rain hiss. Hands become red and sore, cheeks ache in the cold, and there's nothing to do but squint at the drops forming on the end of your nose.

The saddest part about a wet day is that places you have known, places you look forward to seeing again, like Sonning and Shiplake and Wargrave come and go and you can scarcely raise the enthusiasm to turn and look. I remembered Jerome and his friends trying to console each other with noble sentiments about seeing nature in all her moods. But they had the sense to pack up and head for a French supper and a bottle of Beaune at three shillings and sixpence. How gladly I would have joined them, but we were faced by Marsh lock, unattended for the lock keeper was off duty. Instead of sitting around while someone else did the work, we had to get out and open the sluices manually, endlessly winding and winding away at the wheels. There was still some daylight left when we reached Henley, but as far as I was concerned that was it. That was enough for one day.

We woke the next day to a miraculous silence. No rain pattering on the roof, or dripping into puddles. It was actually fine, which was just as well for we had a very, very busy day ahead. I wanted to get off the river that day, which meant that we had to reach Brentford and the lock that would let us into the Grand Union Canal. The Thames is tidal in that reach, so we had to be at the lock not later than two hours after high tide. It was going to be a day for hurrying, with no chance of any kind of stop. But at least a pale sun shone out and we could see what was to be seen: Medmenham Abbey, for example, gothick rather than Gothic, and the home of the notorious Hell-Fire Club, whose way of life was scarcely monastic; and Marlow, where a handsome suspension bridge was built across the river in 1836. Just beyond Marlow lock is a really good, new housing scheme of tall brick houses faced with white weather-boarding, entirely appropriate to their setting. What a marvellous contrast to Bray, where a ghastly block of what the agent's hoarding describes as 'luxury flats' stands by the river. They have just the view they deserve, for they look out on a dull, grey gas holder.

That morning we came out of Cookham lock into the loveliest stretch on the river, a reach that more than makes up for any ugliness you might meet elsewhere along the way. This is Cliveden reach, where the river runs under the shadow of the high Cliveden Hill, thick with trees that reach to the water's edge. Cliveden is really at its best in high summer when the trees are at their lushest, but seen in April, with a light mist touching the water and with the trees in their first Spring greening, it has something of the delicate charm of a Japanese painting. It all ends with the arrival of the river's most famous lock, Boulter's, with its little balustraded bridge. It is still a popular and attractive place, but touched now with an air of melancholy. Boulter's was the perfect spot in the brightest days of Edwardian England, when it was filled with punts and skiffs and men in loud blazers and girls with parasols. Now, one cannot help feeling that its best days are past.

Maidenhead, as far as I'm concerned, is chiefly notable for Brunel's railway bridge which is, of course, on the grand scale. It also presents a very curious optical illusion, which seems to derive from its being built across the river on the skew. As you come towards the bridge it appears to have a quite pronounced slope up from left to right, which is ridiculous because people don't build railway bridges on the incline like that. So you go under the bridge and, lo and behold, it still seems to slope, but in the opposite direction. Very mysterious. There is certainly no shortage of architectural splendours on this stretch of the Thames. Windsor comes up, looking so absurdly hke all the coloured photographs of Windsor that you could take it for a film set; then Eton College, and the amazing red brick of Hampton Court. But brightest of all the memories of the Thames is that of a Thames barge sailing up the wake of a blood red sunset. The day ended with the marvellous swerve around the great bends of Richmond, and with all the excitement of a race which, thanks to the helpful lock keepers, we won and so saved ourselves the long day's wait for the next tide.

As we turned into the canal entrance, past the quay piled high with cargo draped in multi-coloured covers like billowing circus tents, I could have cheered, not just because the race was won, but because I was off the river and back to the canal. You might wonder why, when the river has so many beauties on display. The answer is simple enough – people: not those who work on the river, but those who travel

An old barge on the Thames serves as a reminder that this was once a busy, commercial waterway.

it for pleasure. I had a chat with the old Grand Union lock keeper at Hanwell locks, just north of Brentford. 'River's all right,' he said, 'but I don't get on with the folk. On the canal everyone's ready for a bit of a giggle and a chat. That lot won't even smile at you.' Sadly, there is much truth in that. The river seems to bring out the worst in people – all those weekend Captain Blighs with their nautical hats, ordering their unfortunate families around as though they were in command of the *Queen Mary*: 'Stand by aft! Cast off for'ard!' And they roar up the river without a thought for the little skiffs and the dinghies which they send bobbing in their wakes – river hogs I suppose you'd call them. They're just too grand to care. A couple of ocean-going cruisers came by with bridges as high as a house, and I swear they were actually drinking pink gins in there, just as if they were in a naval wardroom. We were involved in an incident which, for me, summed up the river atmosphere.

We came into a lock and shared it with a fibre-glass cruiser. This was very much a Captain-and-crew boat – they actually seemed to be standing to attention when we came in. Now, we were in a tearing hurry, and we made a mistake: Bill let the bow line off the bollard before we were ready to leave the lock. Several tons of steel hull started to swing out towards the fibre-glass. We received a torrent of deserved abuse, though Bill did not take too kindly to being told to wait for his Captain's orders, and I was not pleased at being instructed to keep my crew under control. I thought of offering to keelhaul them, but there wasn't time. We were in danger of inflicting some damage on the cruiser, and there is no way you can control a stationary boat. So I opened the throttle wide and took the boat out of the lock fast, and the collision was avoided. I got a further torrent of abuse for not waiting my turn.

At the next lock – who goes first makes little difference; you all meet up again at the next lock anyway – I apologized and explained that I was actually being helpful. The apology was most grudgingly accepted but I had to suffer another lecture on discipline. We went into the lock. To my great delight, I noticed that Mrs Bligh was dutifully holding on to the stern line, which went up to the top of the lock, round a bollard and then – nowhere. It had slipped off the cleat and the boat was slowly but surely starting to swing....

CHAPTER 15

London, Back Door and Front

We moored for the night at the foot of Hanwell locks at a spot which we soon discovered to be directly beneath the Heathrow flight path. This was not from choice but from necessity, for we had been warned that a large and cumbersome vessel was to attempt to get up the flight the next day. It was the lock keeper's gloomy forecast that the attempt would fail; it would get stuck, and anyone unfortunate enough to be caught behind it would have to wait until it was unstuck. I had no intention of risking that fate, hence our position poised at the foot of the locks, waiting for the morning opening. We consoled ourselves, as the jumbo jets appeared to be trying to land on the cabin roof, with the thought that at least the weather had changed for the better. That consolation turned out to be based on false assumptions. Morning came as cold as charity, but we did get up, grumbling all the while. After all, you don't expect to be working at eight o'clock on Good Friday morning.

Hanwell is one of those flights you sometimes find in built-up areas which manage to have a really countrified feel about them. In this case the locks run up to the edge of Osterley Park, and that made the early start seem tolerable: that, and the kindness of the friendly lock keeper, who went up ahead to set the locks and ease us on our way, before coming back for a chat. Apart from giving us his views on the Thames, he also passed on a good deal of useful information, some of which I now pass on to those readers who might travel by canal. As we were back on the Grand Union, it was back to broad locks. Now unless you have a big enough crew to have people standing around on the lockside holding ropes, or unless you're sharing a lock, you tend to have a problem stopping the boat from being thrown around by the water. The guaranteed method of solving this difficulty is to line your boat up along one wall of the lock, then open the gate paddle on the opposite side to the boat and the ground paddle on the boat side. Wait until the water covers the sill, then open the second ground paddle. It's as simple as that.

We turned off the main line into the Regent's Canal at Bull's Bridge, where there is a sizeable floating community. It is an area with a good deal of charm, but a charm that was very short-lived, for you turn the corner to run straight into the wastelands of Southall. But once that's behind you, you are very much into back door travel. Places you may have passed a hundred times seem suddenly unfamiliar. The suburban street that seemed all dull conformity at the front presents a wealth of individuality at the back. A few well-known buildings seem to leap at you from out of their surroundings, like the offices of the builders Taylor Woodrow, with the original sculpture from which they get their trade-mark. High up on the wall, a four-man tug-of-war team strains perpetually at the rope, getting nowhere against invisible opponents. I think it was intended as a metaphor for building regulations. Up to the A40, the main London to Oxford road that I'm always travelling on, and the first thing I noticed was the familiar minaret-like tower which belongs so appropriately to the Aladdin company. But under the bridge carrying the four buzzing lanes of traffic there seems to be a world you don't even guess at when you are exercising your neuroses in the rush hour overhead. 'Jackie', the graffiti informed us, 'was knocked up here.' Good Lord, I might have been driving overhead at the time.

Greenford, Horsenden, Alperton and yet another of London's green areas with a large and obviously very popular golf course and some genuine countryside. Horsenden Hill is surrounded by heavily built-up areas such as Ealing and Wembley, but this is no manufactured park, just a bit of country that got left behind by accident, or because it was just a bit too steep to build on with comfort. It is certainly welcome, for we shall be seeing nothing like it for a while now.

Past Alperton, we crossed the North Circular Road. I wish it had been an ordinary working day and not a quiet Good Friday morning. There is nothing more guaranteed to produce a comfortable smugness than chugging at a steady four miles an hour over miles of stationary, fuming, rush hour motorists. Of course, they don't know you are there. I doubt if there are many among the thousands and thousands who use the North Circular every day who have the least idea that there may be a boat passing overhead. They may, perhaps, have wondered why, on a cold winter's morning, one of the bridges over the road drips icicles. I must confess I find a sort of childish fun in being up on that aqueduct. I've got a boat up here, mister, and you don't know. It's hiding up a tree and pulling faces at the passers-by.

Acton Lane Power Station is the next landmark, a gloomy place smothered in cheery notices saying things like 'Danger: 275,000 volts'. Everything is building up, housing is getting denser and denser and industry and railway crowd in so that just for a while you could be back in any industrial city in Britain. Then, quite suddenly, it opens out at Wormwood Scrubs. Was there ever a place with a less lovely name, and was ever name so apt? There is the prison here, which is all most people associate with the place, then a featureless open space for a skyline of tower blocks, with the taller blocks of central London beyond. But turn the other way and a different world appears. Kensal Green Cemetery. How many thousands are buried here in graves marked by simple stones or by the elaborate memorials put up by wealthy Victorians? I am fascinated by this Victorian obsession with the trappings of death. Perhaps it all began with the monarch who spent so many years of her reign in deep mourning. Whatever the reason, they treated the subject, if not with respect, certainly with pomp. No quick slide to the furnace and a cup full of ashes for them. Here, in the graveyard, gloomy figures for ever sit, immobile in their stony grief, their funeral robes falling in frozen cascades while they brood over – who knows who? For the grand, there were the mausoleums, generally in the classical, pagan style always thought peculiarly appropriate to a Christian cemetery. Here and there, stone angels and cherubs poise in dance on the grave heads, a note of optimistic cheerfulness in the general gloom. But all the care, all the effort that went into the monuments have not made

"Blow-up" bridge on the Regent's Canal. It got its name after being rebuilt following the explosion of a gunpowder boat underneath it.

one jot of difference to posterity. The undergrowth has crept up over the graves of the once-loved and Kensal Green is left, a remote, lonely place, slightly sad, rather grand. And to keep it company, the buildings across the canal are tumbling down. Dead people one side, dead buildings the other.

The canal passes under a very fine iron bridge at Harrow Road and then swings away under the great swooping, concrete curve of Westway, flanked by the tall blocks of flats where life at road level must be abject misery. But then, before you have time to adjust to the new scale of modern city life, you're round another corner and into yet another world. Surely this is London's greatest charm? It is not one big city at all, but lots of little places joined together, still preserving their own identities. Little Venice is a place very much possessed of its own identity, even if it has got the wrong name. It has nothing at all in common with the Venetian character. Little Amsterdam would have been far more appropriate. What a contrast, though, with the Paddington towers – from totally undesirable residences at moderate prices to very desirable residences at wildly immoderate prices. And they are desirable, elegant, full of character, and the area shows what can be done when the canal is brought out into the open in the centre of town, made a focal point, and not just hidden behind high brick walls in the hope that it will perhaps just go away.

We had a long wait at Little Venice, as my son Jonathan and his cousin Richard were joining us for the last week of the trip. To while away the time until the train arrived at Paddington, I called on Charles and Alice Mary Hadfield and persuaded them to join us for a drink. Charles is the doyen of canal historians, and we spent a good part of the lunch hour arguing over the relative merits of the canal engineers William Jessop and Thomas Telford, a not infrequent topic of conversation between us. As Charles happens to know more about canals than any one person should decently know, I always feel at something of a disadvantage.

We collected the boys from Paddington, not the most grandiose, but arguably the grandest, of London's stations. It has that sense of breadth and spaciousness you associate with the old Great Western. Brunel's broad gauge demanded it, of course, but the G.W.R. always thought themselves a cut above the rest, and were not going to have anything to do with the vulgar excesses of lesser lines. You can see a railway company's character in its stations, especially in a big London terminus. Sad that the broad gauge remained the odd man out, for if we had it today it might help make the railways more profitable.

It made for good, stable running and spacious carriages. Now it is relegated to the museums.

We set off again with the comfortable feeling that with two healthy teenagers, both experienced canal travellers, on board we could sit back, put our feet up and take a bit of a rest. The section beyond Little Venice has become a popular tourist route in recent years, and deservedly so. You come out of Maida Hill tunnel, under Lisson Grove, topped by a little house, and on into the cutting that takes you round the edge of Regent's Park. At one time they had much grander ideas than that for the canal. The original plan was not for it to go round the park at all, but straight through the middle of it. In fact the route has lost nothing by being left out on the edge. It runs deep in a lovely, leafy cutting which provides a bit of peaceful countryside in central London. It was not quite so peaceful one day in 1874, when a boat loaded with gunpowder blew up under Macclesfield Road bridge. They picked up the pieces of the bridge and put them together again, but in the process they turned the supporting columns the other way round. Look behind those columns and you can still see the old grooves cut by the passing tow ropes of a century ago. The real highlight of this part of the trip is the passage through London Zoo. It was first laid out by Decimus Burton – no family connection – but there is little of the original to be seen now. From the canal the most prominent feature is Lord Snowdon's aviary, which has the great virtue of allowing birds space in which to move, so that you can watch them without suffering too many pangs of guilt over their captivity.

The sun shone, and at Camden lock the holiday crowds swarmed in. This little corner used to be just a wharf at the back end of Camden Town. Now it is a little centre for arts, crafts, antiques and what have you – and none the worse for that. It has brought people down to the canal, and there they stop and gaze at the people passing by in boats. I've never worked a lock with such a large audience before. The old canal men had a marvellous, affectionate name for people who stood around like that, watching others work – gongoozlers. The word's coming back into use a bit on the canal, and hopefully, one day, it will work its way through to more general usage.

Camden Town really marks the end of the tourist's canal, which is a pity, for there is just as much to enjoy as the canal carries on its steady, curving descent towards the river. St Pancras looms over the horizon, that astonishing silhouette of Gothic towers and pinnacles that is the Midland Railway's triumphant proclamation of superiority over older

forms of transport and, so the architects would have you believe, over other railway companies. No wonder people soon began to think of the canals as quaint, old-fashioned things. It is hard to make your voice heard when your next-door neighbour is shouting at the top of his. The Regent's Canal gives up the struggle and goes sulking off into Islington tunnel.

The tunnel marks a strong division. At one end, unfashionable St Pancras; at the other, fashionable Islington. I've never thought Islington was quite the place it was cracked up to be, and I'm inclined to like it less and less as time goes by. A number of writers have pointed out that it suffers from coming a bit too late, looking forward to the stuffy, Victorian respectability of the future rather than back at the lightness and vitality of the Regency. For all that, it is architecturally a lot more pleasant than many another place I could think of in this region. There are two Islingtons now. You can see them in the two markets. Camden Passage started off as a good idea, using the little streets for antique shops and stalls, but it has become chi-chi and expensive, a place where yesterday's garbage enjoys its brief over-priced fling of fashionability before becoming garbage again. Down at the Angel there is the street market, where you can buy decent food at decent prices. It's a polyglot, bustling, shoving, noisy, cheerful sort of place, with no pretensions.

Bill, together with the two boys who had joined us for this part of the trip – the author's son Jon standing and nephew Richard seated at Limehouse Basin.

Where we were, down on the canal, we were lucky. A good whiff of the old Islington still came through, past the expensively renovated terraces. We moored in the deep cutting between the end of the tunnel and City Road locks, and found ourselves in one of those bad news – good news situations. Bad news: all the entrances to the towpath are closed in the early evening, which means your boat is safe from vandals who can't get in, but you can't get out. Good news: if you walk past the locks and under the bridge, you'll find a doorway and an iron staircase, and that staircase leads you right up into the bar of the local pub. They don't come much more convenient than that.

Easter weekend turned out well all round. Next day the sun shone. Not that many boats come this way, and judging by the rubbish that had collected in the locks, we were the first for a good long while. City Basin is another of those sites where development decisions are taken by looking at the balance sheets first and everything else a good deal later. There was a vigorous campaign by those who wanted to use it as a centre for kids to sail and canoe, with other facilities available in one of the old disused commercial buildings. The other proposal was to fill it in and build on it. Today it is just about hanging on, with 'Save City Basin' in faded capitals on a crumbling wall. That same atmosphere stays with you for a good while now. Everywhere you see the old terraces crumbling and the new blocks rising. This is even worse than most places in conveying a sense of continuous decay, for even the older blocks of flats are now dying, and the outdated L.C.C. legend looks as forlorn as 'Save City Basin'.

The mournful mood does not last for ever. Islington goes and Bethnal Green appears. Decay gives way to vitality. There is still a lot of the old East End left here – little streets with little houses; Victoria Park, an open space as fresh and green as any of the more famous central London parks, with its very own, serpentine lake. But a question mark hangs over the area: its character is changing. Already those who are finding Islington a bit too expensive have cast their eyes in this direction. The take-over has begun.

It is a pity the canalside walk scheme does not extend to this part of the canal, for it would arrive at a really splendid, grand finale. We came out of the tight, closed canal world into the wide spaces of Limehouse Basin and Commercial Road Docks. Across the dock, the great gates opened and we slipped, insignificant, into the vast expanses of the ship lock. It seemed almost wilfully prodigal as thousands of gallons of water were poured out just for our benefit and the tiny boat was slowly lowered down to the level of the Thames. The far gates slowly creaked

Leaving Limehouse for the trip up the tidal Thames.

open to give the first, startling glimpse of chopping waves. Then it was throttle open and out into the Pool. Front door London was right there in front of us.

We had taken turns at steering the boat on our tour round Britain but this journey through the heart of London was something that I'd promised myself from the very beginning. This one was for me. And what an experience it was. All around us, the busy river traffic buzzed and chugged. The old trip boat down from Charing Cross pier, rather sedate like an old-fashioned maiden aunt, such a contrast to the new, brash hydrofoils, whipping over the water and hurling up a great wake that had us crashing through the waves while spray flew over the bows. It got even more exciting at Charing Cross Bridge, when one of those sedate ladies suddenly pulled out across our bows in a most unladylike way. That boat started to look very big, very menacing, as I did the watery equivalent of slamming on the brakes, putting the boat into hard reverse so that briefly we wallowed around in the Thames, before slipping comfortably round a stern that seemed as high as an ocean liner's. Somewhere around Hammersmith I finally, and somewhat reluctantly, let someone else take over the tiller. It was only then that I realized how tense I had been. I think I scarcely moved my legs at all. I must have stood there as stiff and immobile as a figurehead stuck at the wrong end of the boat. If I come this way again, no doubt it will all seem tame and ordinary enough, but I shall never forget that first, wonderful trip when the sun shone and everything in the world seemed quite perfect.

And what did I see of London in this trip on London's river? At first, you have no thought for anything but the sheer scale of everything around you. It was not like coming out on to the Trent, where the progression from the old canal was gradual, through steadily widening waterways until you reached the river. Here you left the comfortable puttering of the canal and you were right into it, faced by that great width of water, the traffic, the waves. Once that first shock of size is over, fragmentary impressions creep in. I suddenly noticed the old Prospect of Whitby by Wapping Wall, full of sentimental memories, for I took my wife there on our first date. Tower Bridge – what a marvellous feeling, taking our little canal boat straight up the middle there. I was so elated that I was quite offended they didn't open it for us as we went through. Then the city, the skyline that used to be pierced by the spires ofHawksmoor and Wren, with the dome of St Paul's as the grand culmination. Well, I didn't spend too long looking out over the new city roofs, but turned to the pleasures closer at hand – the marvellous boats lining the river, with the old paddle steamer, the *Caledonian*, setting the standard for elegance. And the bridges come and go. Waterloo Bridge, still one of the handsomest modern bridges I know, and beyond it the South Bank, with its memories of the bravely bright days of the Festival, now pretty well submerged under the great mass of the Hayward Gallery and the National Theatre, as dourly grey as Aberdeen granite. Then the Houses of Parliament, almost absurdly theatrical, but seen quite at their best from the river. From the land they have to compete with the real Gothic across the road. Two modern buildings stand out – the Shell building because it is so crushingly dull, and the Vickers building because it isn't.

Once you are through Lambeth Bridge, you have left central London and the City behind. Of course, there's been too much to take in. London is still one of the great capitals of the world, and you can hardly expect to do it justice in one journey, but I doubt if there is a finer introduction to the place. You start at the port, the trading centre which created the city, pass the commercial heart and then move on to the home of government. Old buildings and new buildings, grimy everyday dockland, gleaming stone of the architectural show places. London is a river city, for it was the river that gave it life.

Past Lambeth, a new London emerges, the London which is as much about where people live as where they work. One side of the river tends to be rather grand as at Cheyne Walk, and even the floating

colony of houseboats at Chelsea Embankment, if not grand, is certainly picturesque. The opposite bank is more workaday – Battersea Power Station, the new fruit and veg. market at Nine Elms, more efficient than the old Covent Garden, but less fun, and the brewery. And the two sides are joined by some splendid bridges, among which Albert Bridge stands supreme. Then, as the river narrows and the traffic eases, the sense of high excitement slackens, and you have time to look out for old friends, like the Doves at Hammersmith, where you get some of the best beer in London. All this slides by in the sun, and quite soon we found ourselves opposite the Brentford eyots and turning off again on to the canal. Our journey on London's river was over.

The Thames at Westminster.

Chapter 16

Home Counties Crawl

We had no intention of repeating the mistake we made last time of mooring at the foot of Hanwell locks, so we stopped right where we were at Brentford. There is a big B.W.B. depot here, and if there was any sense in the world it would be doing ten times the business it is doing. Here you are, on the outskirts of London, with the M4 right on the doorstep. With the new generation of push-pull tugs, containers, BACAT and the rest, there is an ideal opportunity to create a new port complex on the edge of town. Just think of all those heavy lorries that now have to trundle through central London to reach the docks; think of the time and money lost in traffic snarl-ups. Even if you consider that preserving the sanity of Londoners is a matter of little importance, you have to admit that the economic arguments make this a scheme worth developing. But, to be honest, such serious matters were not foremost in my mind, for we had heard rumours of a delightful little sailors' pub called the Brewer's Tap, which was said to sell Fuller's beer and be worth visiting. Rumour, for once, did not lie.

The next day was guest day, and we had arranged to pick up friends at eleven o'clock at Bull's Bridge. We seemed to have ample time, but we had not allowed for the Easter weekend traffic jam at Hanwell. Two days ago we had fairly zipped up the locks, but now we found that the world and his wife were there as well. We had got so used to moving at our own pace, we had quite forgotten that there were going to be an awful lot of people around from now on. We were quite literally beset by hold-ups. Our friendly lock keeper was on the scene and I had just opened the paddles to let a boat down the lock and was chatting amicably when we heard anguished cries from the man at the tiller. He had passed a rope up round the bollard and then tied the other end to his boat. Of course, as the boat went down the knot tightened, and he found himself suspended from the lock side. We hurriedly wound down the paddles and began to refill the lock. It was not that quick a process. These locks have hydraulic gears – thirty-six turns of the handle to get them down, thirty-six turns to get the others up, not like the old paddles that can be dropped in a second in an emergency. He was lucky there was no great damage done. These new gears are not only ugly, rotten to use and expensive to maintain, but also dangerous.

The Grand Union Canal climbing up from the Thames via Hanwell locks.

Exactly the same thing happened to another boat a few days later. The lock keeper's view on the monstrosities was succinct: 'If they'd asked any lock keeper, he'd have told 'em they were bloody daft.'

Eventually, and very belatedly, we picked up our passengers and made our somewhat dreary way through the outer suburbs, acres of housing with a spattering of light industry, an amorphous smear spreading out from central London. The canal provides a welcome note of relief, and people obviously enjoy it. Every lock was ringed with gongoozlers who came to watch the strange sight of boats going up and down the watery lifts, while the amateur crews bustled around, with varying degrees of competence. I never mind providing a little free entertainment and, Heaven knows, there seems to be little enough to enjoy when you look away from the canal. We were back with the lock closures, so we had no time to stop. But we did manage to get in a pint as we came up to the lock at Cowley and get glasses back to the bar by the time we were out again at the top. We got that technique down to a fine art during the rest of the week.

Suburbia ends quite abruptly at Uxbridge, with the A40 marking the boundary. You come up to the road bridge and there, under the angular span, you can see the familiar, white-washed, hump-backed canal bridge. This is the Colne valley, an area well marked by generations of settlers, especially the mill owners who diverted the river water to turn their wheels. The mills and the mill ponds still stand by the cut. Today, we see them as romantic places. We enjoy the sight of them, the tall weather-boarded fronts, the covered hoists, the regular rhythm of arched windows set into ageing brick walls. We like to watch the water run by the wheel pit, even if the wheel itself has long since gone. Mills are not the only marks left on the land. All along the route the watercress beds can be seen and, close by them, the somewhat uglier gaps where man has taken what he needs from the land – the chalk quarries and gravel pits. The gravel pit is rather like the spoil heap. No matter what you do with it, it remains a totally unnatural shape in the land. Even when you reclaim it and use it for fun and leisure as they've done with the aquadrome at Rickmansworth, it still continues to look like a gravel pit. But it's a great improvement, for all that: a centre for all kinds of sports, water skiing, boating, swimming or just a stretch of water for people to walk around. It is simply a place to enjoy.

Rickmansworth itself seems to suffer from a badly split personality. Start at the water with the aquadrome and the canal, the area around the lock where people can stand and watch others like us slave away, making idiots of ourselves. Here the cottages by the bridge form an

attractive group and beyond them is the lock house, isolated on its own little island. Then, just a short distance away, there is the church and a row of shops and houses. But walk on and you meet the roads, the through route built up above town level, with a big intersection dipping down towards it. It all writes finis, makes a dead end to the old town, relegates it to second place in the scale of importance. That road has made a new Rickmansworth, for most people here have few allegiances to the place. It's just a dormitory, somewhere to lay your head before you have to be off down that road or the nearby rails to London, for that's where the real centre of Rickmansworth lies now.

After Rickmansworth, you leave the Colne for the Gade Valley. It was a sunny Easter Monday when we set off for a day of frustrations and delights: delight in some truly splendid country, frustration from a crowded waterway and those wretched time restrictions. We got off to a good start, first in the queue at ten o'clock when the lock opened. We squeezed in with two other boats, then we were away to one of those irritating staggers of locks, where you are for ever hopping in and out of the boat.

The frustrations don't last and the pleasures more than compensated. Cassiobury Park has to come high up on the list. The British have a genius for creating parkland that combines the best of natural countryside with the comfortable feeling that man has, after all, got his environment well under control. It is a tamed wilderness. These old

Brentford depot: at this date there was still a steady commercial trade for Thames lighters.

parks are, by their very nature, optimistic places, for they were created by supremely optimistic individuals. Who but the most optimistic would go to the trouble and expense of planting an avenue of limes which would only grow to maturity long after the planter's death? You have to believe that your sort of world will survive, that your descendants will want and appreciate what you want and appreciate. The limes, which once formed an avenue for courtly promenades by the Earl of Sussex and his retinue, have passed the two-centuries mark and are still appreciated. Our canal was a late addition to the park, but it does its best to fit in with the character of the place. You don't normally associate the Grand Union with aimless meanderings, but in the open parkland it twists and bends around, so that it seems to shed all its artificial character. And at the Grove it is crossed by a fine, low, ornamental bridge. There is a lovely sweeping curve to the parapet, which is supported by shapely balustrading. The park ends at Grove Mill, which has been converted for housing and, seen from the outside, very well converted at that, keeping the original character of the building. Mills are such a feature of the canalside scene in this part of the world that one particular mill could well slip by without special comment, but at King's Langley happy accident has got together all the right elements and held them in a perfect balance – the tall block of the mill, the strong horizontals of the balance beam and the fresh, green, falling curves of the willow on the bank.

Each generation has to find its own solutions to problems such as transport, though quite often these turn out to be no more than the old problems grown bigger or given a new twist. The canal forms one of the three routes forced into the valley that cuts through the hills to the north of London. Road, rail and canal – all were fixed by the same geographical constraints, and by the need to serve the string of settlements that found comfortable shelter under the lee of those hills. You don't see very much of the road from the canal, though you see – and hear – a good deal of the railway, but later in the evening I wandered over to take a look at the main road. In the past, roads needed coaching inns, with rooms for travellers and stables for their horses. Now the motorist wants a room for himself and a garage for his car. The motel has taken over from the coaching inn, but there is no real change. They both fulfil the same function. At Bourne End, a mill has been adapted and enlarged to meet the new requirements, and very well it has been done too. The style of the new fits the style of the old; brick and weather-boarding, appropriate to the building and to the area. But there are other building materials to be found in these parts.

Scuff up a bit of ground and you'll turn up flint, and if you have a sense of curiosity you might start looking around for a flint building. You'd find one soon enough, a little flint cobble church down in the valley, not far from the motel. Lovely little place, it is. The tiny church, with its spire in exact balance with the nave, may not be in anyone's list of great buildings, but it is as satisfying as any grand building simply because it is so right, so at home in its setting.

Along the way we met a young couple and their boat, the new generation of waterway residents, not working boat families but nomads. There are quite a few now who have taken to the idea of a mobile, floating home. On the back of the boat was a little handwritten placard, announcing 'JUST MARRIED'. She was like a Victorian waif, long skirt brushing her bare feet and 'Bubbles' hair cut. He was the suburban mum's nightmare – close cropped hair, tattooed arms and a bruised face that did not suggest he'd accidentally walked into a door. The unlikely pair went their own way, totally unaware of the world around them.

The first town we met next day was Berkhamsted, another in the string of towns and villages popping up along the line of the main valley road. There is a general rule you can apply: the amount of individuality a town retains is directly proportional to its distance from London. Berkhamsted is a decent distance away and presents a pleasing and rather urbane face to the world, a hotch-potch of styles and periods that somehow manage to blend together into a satisfactory whole. It boasts a castle, ruined; a church of styles, various, almshouses and a lovely railway station that has escaped modernization. Sadly, as one leaves the town proper one comes up to the ribbon development that spreads down a valley with gently sloping hills and woods, where our ancestors once sensibly tucked their towns away in folds and hollows.

At Dodswell locks we entered the great and famous Tring Development Scheme. The whole scheme is, and I quote the official documents, 'a shop window', a place where people can see for themselves how a canal should look.' I looked, and what I saw was that a perfectly sound towpath had been replaced by a gravel walk. The larger stones have long since found their way into the cut, leaving a fine grit which swirled in the wind in passable imitation of a Saharan sandstorm. I looked, and saw the gaps where mature beech and ash have been felled and I looked at the poor spindly creatures that have been planted in their places, already sadly depleted by vandalism. I looked, at the overpruned hedgerows and the metal strip that now keeps the edge of the canal neat and tidy. And then I looked away again, and moved off towards the rich, untidy world of Tring cutting, where the canal forces its way through the swelling ground of the Chilterns.

The sun blazed overhead, and the cutting was at peace, with only the cries of birds to accompany the rhythmic beat of the engine. It seemed as if we were intruders, for the water was still, the sense of remoteness from the busy world complete. The birds thought so. A kingfisher, a darting arrow of electric blue, flashed down to the water, then rose sharply up to perch again among the pale green leaves. We kept on coming towards him, so he shot off again to take a new stance further down the cutting. We kept on, and at last he gave up the game and sat morosely in his tree, puffing out his bright red chest as we moved beneath him. The cutting here is very similar to the deep cuttings of the Shropshire Union, but now we were feeling spring all around us. The thick grey tangles of branches were touched with spots, then whole wide masses of green. Buds stood thick and swollen on the branches. Catkins drooped over the water. I could have travelled through such peace all day, but if I had to emerge, what better scene to come out to than Marsworth?

The first thing you see when you leave the cutting is Bulbourne Yard. One of the few virtues of the Tring scheme has been the work done on buildings such as these. Here the work has been aimed not at providing false trappings, but at bringing out the essential qualities that were always there, hidden behind the grime of years. It is a simple, functional sort of place, the only concession to luxury being the ornate clock tower,

topped by a weather-vane. Even that was not really a piece of frivolity, for the canal age was an age when clocks were rare and the clearly visible timepiece was an important part of the working day. Down from Bulbourne, in a great series of sweeping bends, go the Marsworth locks. Because of the restrictions, we had been keeping a second boat company for the last couple of days, and we set off to go down Marsworth breasted up. This is not some bizarre fetish but a method of travelling in which the two boats are tied together, side by side, so that they can be steered in and out of the locks as one. It saves a lot of time and bother, and is really rather fun, especially if the two steerers try and go in opposite directions. The canal bends round the Marsworth reservoirs, and it is amazing how these particular artificial stretches of water have blended into the landscape. This is largely because of the reed beds that have grown out from the side and softened the hard, artificial outline. This area is a bird sanctuary now, but the one time that I came here to look at the birds, I was scared half out of my wits. It was summer and the swallows had taken over, diving like *kami-kaze* pilots straight at the top of my head. I beat a rapid retreat.

We eventually stopped at Ivinghoe bridge, just beyond Seabrook locks. I chatted for a while to the young lock keeper and his wife, refugees from London and just finishing their first two months' work on the canal. He'd got his own length of canal to look after, and a pleasant little cottage by the water. You could say he was getting all the year round what other people spend a fortune to get for a weekend. He

Marsworth locks mark the beginning of the drop down from the summit level of the Grand Union.

also had to work hard, in all weathers, for lousy pay, but still reckoned he had the best of the bargain.

Ivinghoe is a village set in a very natural site. Here the Chilterns end, marked by the old hill fort of Ivinghoe Beacon. Hills meant safety but, with time, comfort seemed to become more important so the villagers shifted down into a sheltered fold in the hillside, out of the weather, and here the village of Ivinghoe grew. And grow is just what it did do, for, apart from a council estate tacked on in one solid lump, the village shows all the rich diversity that comes from slow, unhurried change. Urbane Georgian dignity acts as a foil to the rough Tudor squatting down beside it. The older house seems to peer suspiciously, and a little myopically, through the tiny leaded windows, up at the broad, wide-awake gaze of its more modern neighbour. I was happy wandering around the village, peering in at the church, looking at the old windmill, but Phil was even happier, for this was home territory to him. This was where he spent his childhood. We joined him on a nostalgic pilgrimage to his old home, then we retired to the pub for a farewell drink with our companions of the last few days. It was slightly sad, for they were turning back for home and it was a reminder that we too were on the last stage of the journey.

The cast iron trough aqueduct at Cosworth.

CHAPTER 17

Journey's End

We awoke happy in the knowledge that we had only to get through Fenny Stratford lock, a mere fourteen miles away and we could look forward to another eleven miles beyond that without a lock and therefore without a restriction. We could enjoy a full day's travel.

The day began in a minor key. Wide, flat grassland had taken over from the swelling hills. The locks that had come together in clumps as we came down the slope were now spaced out over wide intervals. Some sections of canal come as short statements, full of stops, with lots of action – Hemingway canals you could call them; on others you meander for a very long time, with just the occasional visual comma, and long waits before the next stop. That was what we had – a Henry James canal.

There was plenty of time to look around, read the landscape and take in its finer points. One place did stand out from the rest. At Church lock stands the tiny parish church which gives it its name. But where is the parish? A pleasant, teasing little mystery. Leighton Buzzard announces its presence with its great spire, but the canal nips round the edge of the town and it's gone before you are quite aware of what has happened, and suddenly you are at Leighton lock. Out the other side, and the town is just a memory. Over on the right bank woodland began to cover the rising ground – not the regimented pines so beloved of the Forestry Commission, but the old mixed woods with more shades of green than any artist could mix on his palette. We passed, sadly, the Globe at Linslade, just the sort of pub such a setting deserves, with thatched roof and benches set against the wall for you to sit on in beery comfort and watch the boats go by. After that the manor farm, with its castellated church close at hand, set proprietorially among the rich pastures. Through this pleasant land to Soulbury, where three locks give you comfortable time to get a pint down while you work. Then you reach Bletchley through that last lock, and you find a new world waiting for you.

Look at most maps and you will still see nothing but a spattering of small villages, but those villages are being steadily surrounded and linked. We had reached Milton Keynes, which must surely be one of the most exciting projects that the country has seen in this century.

We have had city redevelopment, we have had complete new towns – but now we are to have a new city. That is a daunting prospect. For a city is something more than just another big town, more, even, than the centre of a region. The city has a special ethos, stands in a great tradition. The officials can plan for a super-estate with offices here, factories there, shops somewhere else and houses clustered round the outside – or they can produce somewhere that will have a chance to grow with the centuries, to develop a character of its own. Your first glimpse of Milton Keynes might make you fear the worst. The approach roads converge under ominously Orwellian signs, announcing that you are approaching M7 or C4, references to the complex city grid. You get the feeling that movement in this new city is going to be like a game of chess, B to K4, Q to Kt3. But get beyond that chilling nomenclature, and you begin to find something quite different. From my admittedly limited view on the canal, I kept getting this feeling of vigour and excitement. Time and again, I saw something happening which seemed to say: here are people using their imaginations, really trying to create a city that would not be ashamed to see itself in a list that includes York, Chester and Oxford, not to mention Bristol, Liverpool or Leeds.

It would have been easy to lose sight of the ageing canal in the enthusiasm for new roads and new buildings, but in Milton Keynes they have actually had the sense to see it as a positive asset, a ready-made axis around which parkland and all kinds of amenities can be grouped. And what is even more impressive is the way in which the planners are doing this by reinforcing the qualities the canal already has, not by trying to turn it into a pretty-pretty stream or a long duckpond. Old bridges are being refurbished with the right materials; the towpath has been improved for walking, not by scattering gravel but by impacting stone to make a really solid surface. And they've found a new use for old buildings, turning a small wharf warehouse into a youth club. All right, Milton Keynes is not going to be judged by how it treats the canal that happens to run through it, but I would say that this is just the sort of thing that is absolutely vital to the future of the city. If the planners can take this much care over what is, admittedly, a minor part of the whole scheme, then there is a real hope that that whole can be a success.

It is housing that you see mostly from the canal, with just occasional glimpses of offices and factories, and what I could see of the housing reinforced my favourable impression. How very good to see traditional materials coming back into favour, especially brick. The bricks may not be what they would have been a century ago, but the best of the

A **pair** of former working narrow boats at Buckby locks: the motor boat is on the left and the unpowered butty on the right.

modern bricks really do have a look of richness about them. One group of red brick houses caught my eye and seemed to exemplify the concern for quality in Milton Keynes. They were set in a hollow which had obviously been excavated, and the bank that had been built up around them was grassy and bright with a haphazard scattering of spring flowers. A brick wall at the back did close the houses off from the canal, but it was not a total enclosure. You could easily wander through to the tree-lined walk by the water. What really impressed me was the overall layout, the ground plan of the group. You see so many estates just plonked down: draw a fine, road here, houses there, front garden, back garden, garage, plonk, plonk, plonk. Here you feel they have asked questions like: where are the kids going to play? Do we need any special facilities? The houses seem to be there for people, not profit, first.

Once you start building well, it's catching. You can't sell rubbish if there is something better down the road – a theory that, I must admit, owes more to native optimism than hard evidence. But there was some corroboration further on at Linford Wharf, where a group of houses built round a square managed to look traditional and modern at the same time – modern design, traditional materials. At ground level, a white-arched door stood out from a dark wall, while above the effect was even more dramatic, with windows and a sparkling white-louvred opening in stark contrast to creosoted weather-boarding, the whole topped by a dark, tiled roof. The design was bold, almost startling, yet at the same time, the obvious echoes of warehouses and mills made the group seem quite at home by the water. After that, it was a disappointment to find a lovely old Dutch-gabled house simply abandoned and semi-derelict: an awful waste. It was even more of a disappointment to leave exciting new developments and come back to the familiar clumps of housing estates that cluster round Wolverton.

Wolverton, though, was not the end of the day. We came out on the other side for one of those marvellous experiences which are unique to the canal. We crossed the Ouse on an iron trough aqueduct. There used to be a brick aqueduct here, but it fell down and the new structure took its place. For people walking around the countryside, there is no doubt that a fine arched stone or brick aqueduct is a more pleasing sight than what is really just an open iron box full of water stuck up on pillars. (The one great and glorious exception is the Pont Cysyllte, near Llangollen.) But, for the traveller by boat, the iron trough wins every time. The thing is that the edge of the trough is just a metal plate and as it is lower than the side of the boat, you simply cannot see it at all. It is an eerie sensation to be floating, apparently unsupported, high over the river, above the tops of trees.

Beyond the aqueduct, Cosgrove and closures. All day we had followed a pair of working boats, the motor boat in front, the second boat, the butty, towed behind. These were Grand Union Canal Carrying Company boats that shift coal around the country all winter, and in summer are hired out as camping boats. Dozens of kids can sleep under the boats' canvases. The motor boat had a professional steerer, old Alec. He was born on the cut, his family were born on the cut, he spent all his working life on the cut and now, in retirement, he still comes back each summer. If the words 'old' and 'retired' suggest some doddering character scarcely able to lift pen to pension book, forget it. I'd as soon walk into the ring with Mohammed Ali as start a quarrel with old Alec. So I didn't start a quarrel; just spent some happy hours listening to the talk of the old days and downing a few ales.

Alec's generation of boatmen lived in a world of their own, with its own rules and its own language. Look in the canal guides and you'll find names for all the locks – and Alec wouldn't recognize one of them. The old boatmen had their own names, and he can rattle them off, every lock from Birmingham to London. It was a different world all right, and no wonder they laugh at the pretensions of us amateur boatmen as we talk about good runs, when he can recall doing the run down from Brummagem in forty-eight hours. It was a hard world, and it could be a violent one. It was one of those very old-fashioned societies, where men took a pride in physical prowess, and showed it. Alec can tell you tales in plenty about his fights. He'll tell you about the time he was knocked cold, was taken for dead and woke to find he'd been sewn up in a canvas bag. Once you had a reputation, you were always liable to be challenged. He tells another story about the time he was goaded, reluctantly, he said, into a fight. He started to clamber out of his boat to take up the challenge and the other bloke put a boot in his face. That cost Alec his front teeth and it made him a bit angry. In the end it cost the other fellow 84 stitches to close up the wounds Alec made with his bare fists. Hard fighting, hard boozing – that was the order of the day. Tall stories, too, you might think. Did he really get down 28 pints one lunch time? I don't know, but I wasn't going to argue about it with Alec.

Next day we were again free of time pressures. The locks at Stoke Bruerne were only six miles away, and we could obviously clear those with ease, but the next set were over twenty miles beyond that and there was no way we could get through them in the six hours between closures. So we pottered along a route that wavered and weaved through an amazingly empty countryside. Villages were distant from the canal, and only the little River Tove ran alongside to keep us company. It was just as well we were not in any hurry for the closures cause traffic jams, and Stoke locks were a scene of almost lunatic activity. There are only seven of the things, but it took us an hour and a half to get up, working behind Alec and his pair of boats. It was worth waiting.

Stoke Bruerne has become something of a tourist attraction. Beyond the handsome double-arched bridge is the Waterways Museum, a lovely row of cottages, locks – and a fine old thatched pub, the Boat. That was the goal. For the past week we had had to trundle past splendid lunch stops or just snatch a quick one as we went through a lock. Now we had time, and the promise of good, real ale. All the way up, Phil had been muttering the name 'Ruddles', like a magic incantation. Then I got to the bar, only to be told by the landlord that it was off, sold out over Easter. I asked him if he actually enjoyed the sight of grown men weeping on his doorstep, at which point he informed me that though the Ruddles was off, the Marston's was on. That was a great consolation. It was a good long while and a few pints before we got under way again, past a whole fleet of narrow boats. Then I steered the boat cheerfully, if somewhat waveringly, though the 3,000 yards of darkness that is Blisworth tunnel. As we zipped through I regaled the company with a selection from my extensive vocal repertoire. They responded, I am sorry to say, by throwing things, which illustrates the depths of ingratitude to which mankind can sink. Half an hour later we were out into the light and my voice had to compete with the empty hoo-hooing of the wood pigeons, the club bores of the bird world.

We eventually stopped just outside Weedon. It is one of those places that I know slightly. On my way home from the north, I often turn off the M1 near here and drive through the town. It had never seemed very interesting, held out few promises. But six weeks on the canal had at least taught me one thing: the town with no features of interest at all probably does not exist. (I dare say I could even find them in Nuneaton, if I looked hard enough.) Weedon turned out to be very much more fascinating than I could ever have guessed. We came into the town on a high bank, and the railway does the same, with the result that the poor little church is incongruously sandwiched between the two, as uncomfortable as one of those meek httle men squashed between two vast women on a seaside postcard. All you can see from the boat is the top of the tower, but beyond that you can catch a glimpse of the distant blocks and towers of Weedon barracks.

We walked across to see the barracks, which were built at the time of the Napoleonic wars when invasion from France was threatened. They used to be much more extensive than they are today. There were no less than three royal pavilions for King George to hide away in, in suitably royal comfort. Why Weedon? Well, it is about as far as you can get from a sea port, so, logically, it should be the last place an invading army could reach. There is not a good deal left, but what there is is ranged, with true military precision, around an arm of the canal, for the canal was to be the main supply line for this last-stand fortress. Even here the military presence dominates, and this must surely be the only canal to be closed off by a portcullis. Rigidly ordered the barracks may be, but there is a frivolous, unmilitary little cupola over the main entrance.

This was to be the last evening in the last canal pub, so we headed for the Narrow Boat. I spent most of the night chatting to a young couple who run another pair of G.U.C.C.C. boats, and in a way they represented the new generation that is so different from that of old Alec and his friends. I suppose you could call them drop-outs, and he certainly looked the part with dark hair halfway down his back and a heavy *banditti* moustache. But if working boats in all seasons and all weathers is dropping out, then it's a damned hard drop. Yet in one sense, they are no different from Alec. They are looking for independence, a life where the pace is still human and under their own control where hard work is rewarded with a satisfaction that does not just come from the pay packet. You cannot dismiss such attitudes as romantic nonsense. Why else should Alec come back every year? It is certainly not for the money. Maybe they are living at the fag-end of a dying age, though there are promises of new cargoes, a regular grain run to Anderton that will see them through next winter and maybe longer. Perhaps the old days are gone for ever, and they are going to spend more and more of their time ferrying parties of kids. They accept that: it is the price they are happy to pay. Their only complaint about the kids is that so many of them seem to suffer from built in conventionality. They are constantly being asked. Don't you want a real house? Don't you want to settle down?

The night ended. Alec offered Phil a fight to prove he was still as strong as ever, and Phil wisely refused. We all parted on good terms. Next morning we set off on what was, unbelievably, the last day. We chugged up to Whilton locks and the inevitable queue and waited as the traffic sorted itself out. The morning run was a gentle saunter through pleasant woodland. In the gaps, one could see the fields with little tightly knotted coppices, and tall beech and oak rising from the hedgerows. A fine land, and only yards away is the M1 with its hustling traffic. How many times have I come this way and never registered the beauties of the scene? Not surprising, perhaps, for this is a landscape that demands time. There is no obvious focal point, just the steadily changing patterns as you move slowly by and the trees shift in relation to each other with steady rhythm. Drive through the country, and all you see are the big, four-star attractions, the tall hill, the cliff, the forest. There is no time to take in the delicate interlacing of branches against the sky; no time to catch the one perfect moment when everything comes together in an astonishing harmony, when, with a dry rattle, the reeds sway and bow at the water's edge, striking the one curve that was needed to balance the tall rise of a tree's stem. It had taken a long time for the rhythm of my life to match the slow pace of the land.

Too soon now we reached Braunston tunnel, just over a mile long and notably untrue. Those subterraneous kinks can pose a real hazard to a full-length boat. But we slid easily through. Out into the light and a microcosm of the canal world today. To the left was the old canal bridge, with its 'Ladyline' advert, and beyond the bridge was the new marina, full of fibre-glass cruisers. Down the length of the cut, the working boats were moored. *Lynx* and *Jaguar* and the rest, boats we had met before on our travels. It was the old world and the new, and the old is going fast. We turned away, back up the canal we had travelled six weeks and nine hundred miles before. The new lambs that had tottered, wobbling, after mother were now plumped out, stolid, dully sheepish. The branches that had been dry, grey sticks were bright with fresh leaves and their first blossoming. Even the canal had changed. Now it was lower, muddier, busy with traffic where once we had made our solitary way. So it was back to Hillmorton, back to the car and the journey home.

It is amazing how quickly the old ways take over again. Cars are made to go fast, so you go fast. The world whips by unnoticed. But on the signposts, familiar names come and go – Napton, Fenny Compton, Claydon, then, just minutes later, Banbury; did that journey from Claydon to Banbury really take us five hours only two weeks ago? Turn off the main road, over the Oxford Canal by the Rock of Gibraltar, and home. The children have hung up a notice -'Welcome Home Dad'. The journey was really over. It was done. Next day I should wake with no boat to move on. I should see no one's back door but my own.

Index